A Year in the Life of the

Great Western

60

A Year in the Life of the Great Western

Tim Bryan

For Pat and Winifred

First published 2015

ISBN 978 0 7110 3802 8

Published by Ian Allan Publishing Ltd, Addlestone, Surrey KT12 2SF

Printed in Bulgaria

Visit the Ian Allan Publishing website at *www.ianallanpublishing.com*

Picture credits
Every effort has been made to identify and correctly attribute photographic credits. Should any error have occurred, this is entirely unintentional. Individual picture sources are noted within the text. All uncredited images are from the collection of STEAM – Museum of the GWR. Further images from the museum's picture library can be viewed at www.steampicturelibrary.com

FRONT COVER **Cab view of an identified GWR 'Castle', 1951.** *Ian Allan Library*

BACK COVER **Goods depot at Bristol in the 1920s (see page 44).**

HALF TITLE PAGE **'45xx' 2-6-2T No 4512 heads away from the terminus at St Ives in the 1930s.**

HALF TITLE VERSO **Flagship of the GWR locomotive fleet, 4-6-0 No 6000 *King George V* is pictured at Swindon on 5 June 1927.**

TITLE PAGE **A very tall gas lamp dominates this view of a GWR goods yard; in the background yard staff await the arrival of a train and a shunter stands ready armed with his shunter's pole.**

CONTENTS

FOREWORD

Although many of the books written about the Great Western Railway and its operations have taken a broadly chronological or historical approach this book instead provides the reader with a different perspective, presenting a portrait of the operation of the railway throughout a typical year. It is, of course, something of an oversimplification to say that there was no such thing as a 'typical' year on the Great Western, and even the most cursory glance at the history of the company reveals that it faced vastly different challenges and problems over the course of every year of its 148-year existence. To provide some historical continuity and focus, however, the book largely records the 'year-round' activities of the GWR in the period between the two world wars, with a few specific references to events before and after these conflicts.

Rather than concentrating on the bigger issues faced by the GWR in the 1920s and 1930s this book looks instead at the day-to-day activities of the railway through the seasons in that period. As a result it can be seen as a companion to my book *The Inheritance — The GWR between the Wars*, published in 2013, which provided a broader historical narrative to what was a turbulent and challenging period in the history of the company.

For those employed by the Great Western, the working year tended to follow a well-worn and familiar pattern. Many GWR employees of this period had spent their whole working lives in

BELOW An unidentified 'Castle' 4-6-0 speeds westward between Dawlish and Teignmouth with a down express.

the service of the company, so with the exception of the years dominated by the two world wars there was a natural annual routine with which most staff were very familiar. From the long dark nights and poor weather of winter to the coming of spring and start of summer services staff normally measured their year by the run-up to the busiest time of the year, the holiday season. With the rush and heat of the holidays over the railway then settled back into a somewhat quieter routine in the months before the hectic Christmas period, although its excursion and freight business remained busy all year round, as always.

Using the seasonal calendar to describe the work done by the railway over the course of a year is not a precise science, as one season tends to blend gradually to the next, and while some readers may argue with my interpretation of seasonal change, looking at the operation of the railway over the course of a year nevertheless provides an understanding of what made the company and its staff so resilient and successful despite all the challenges it faced. It must also be remembered that some of the services and activities run by the GWR were not confined to one part of the year, but in some cases particular aspects of the story have been described in a particular section of the book to provide a spread of activities through the railway's year. Three further chapters highlight some of the year-round activities undertaken by the GWR — its handling of milk traffic, its freight business and, finally, its hotel and refreshment-room operation.

Wherever possible the seasonal story for the railway has been told through the use of company records and publicity. At least some inspiration for the book has been drawn from the 'Bristol Diaries', a unique set of bound volumes preserved in the National Archives. Compiled by the GWR Divisional Superintendent at Bristol between 1913 and 1948, each volume contains official reports, press cuttings, handbills and other material that give a real insight into the work of the railway during this period. The book also draws on other company records, official timetables and publications and the

ABOVE **Staff unloading cattle at a country station in 1936. The photograph was taken to publicise the company's farm-removal service.**

BELOW **The railway calendar reproduced in the GWR publication *Speed to the West* in 1939.**

SPRING, SUMMER,
AUTUMN or WINTER—

WEST IS BEST!

CALENDAR, 1939.

	JANUARY	FEBRUARY	MARCH
S	1 8 15 22 29	– 5 12 19 26	– 5 12 19 26
M	2 9 16 23 30	– 6 13 20 27	– 6 13 20 27
Tu	3 10 17 24 31	– 7 14 21 28	– 7 14 21 28
W	4 11 18 25 –	1 8 15 22 –	1 8 15 22 29
Th	5 12 19 26 –	2 9 16 23 –	2 9 16 23 30
F	6 13 20 27 –	3 10 17 24 –	3 10 17 24 31
S	7 14 21 28 –	4 11 18 25 –	4 11 18 25 –

	APRIL	MAY	JUNE
S	– 2 9 16 23 30	– 7 14 21 28 –	– 4 11 18 25
M	– 3 10 17 24 –	1 8 15 22 29 –	– 5 12 19 26
Tu	– 4 11 18 25 –	2 9 16 23 30 –	– 6 13 20 27
W	– 5 12 19 26 –	3 10 17 24 31 –	– 7 14 21 28
Th	– 6 13 20 27 –	4 11 18 25 – –	1 8 15 22 29
F	– 7 14 21 28 –	5 12 19 26 – –	2 9 16 23 30
S	1 8 15 22 29 –	6 13 20 27 – –	3 10 17 24 –

	JULY	AUGUST	SEPTEMBER
S	– 2 9 16 23 30	– 6 13 20 27	– 3 10 17 24
M	– 3 10 17 24 31	– 7 14 21 28	– 4 11 18 25
Tu	– 4 11 18 25 –	1 8 15 22 29	– 5 12 19 26
W	– 5 12 19 26 –	2 9 16 23 30	– 6 13 20 27
Th	– 6 13 20 27 –	3 10 17 24 31	– 7 14 21 28
F	– 7 14 21 28 –	4 11 18 25 –	1 8 15 22 29
S	1 8 15 22 29 –	5 12 19 26 –	2 9 16 23 30

	OCTOBER	NOVEMBER	DECEMBER
S	1 8 15 22 29	– 5 12 19 26	– 3 10 17 24 31
M	2 9 16 23 30	– 6 13 20 27	– 4 11 18 25 –
Tu	3 10 17 24 31	– 7 14 21 28	– 5 12 19 26 –
W	4 11 18 25 –	1 8 15 22 29	– 6 13 20 27 –
Th	5 12 19 26 –	2 9 16 23 30	– 7 14 21 28 –
F	6 13 20 27 –	3 10 17 24 –	1 8 15 22 29 –
S	7 14 21 28 –	4 11 18 25 –	2 9 16 23 30 –

BANK HOLIDAYS ·· 1939

Easter Monday, April 10th
Whit Monday, May 29th
Monday, August 7th
Boxing Day, Tuesday, December 26th

Great Western Railway Magazine, which reported monthly on the activities of the company and its employees.

It is something of a cliché to argue that a book such as this provides us with a window into a world very different from the one we know today. Nevertheless, looking back at the way in which the GWR operated through the year in the 1920s and 1930s one finds it hard to avoid the conclusion that modern technology has reduced the impact of the seasons on our lives. While winter weather can still wreak havoc on the railway system now, as it did then, changes in holiday and working patterns have reduced the impact of summer traffic for train companies, as people now take breaks all year round. Cheap air travel has, of course, also opened up many new destinations for holidaymakers, and air freight has provided consumers with access to all manner of fresh produce from overseas that was previously available only during specific seasons in Britain.

Inevitably, in describing the activities of Great Western staff in the years between the two world wars, this book and its photographs show working practices and operations that despite the impact and consequences of the Second World War would continue well into the 1950's when the GWR became the Western region of British Railways. The subsequent BR Modernisation Plan and the Beeching Report marked the end of an era when railways were, for many at least, still the only way to travel long distances for business or pleasure and a period when the scope and impact of railways like the Great Western were enormous, covering not only the operation of passenger and goods trains, but also road transport, docks, shipping, refreshment rooms and hotels.

ABOVE Staff from the GWR's removal service carefully unload a kitchen cabinet from a container in 1935. The container has been delivered by a company-owned Scammell Mechanical Horse.

RIGHT This 1936 Frank Newbould poster was based on the Cornish fishing village of Polperro. *Great Western Trust collection*

Tim Bryan
Swindon
May 2015

FRANK NEWBOULD
CORNWALL
GWR

INTRODUCTION

The beginning of a new year is naturally an opportunity not only to celebrate but also to reflect on the past 12 months and to look forward to the year ahead. As GWR General Manager Felix Pole noted in 1924, the New Year was the chance to 'forecast the prospects of the future, to gauge the promise of good fortune and wish everyone around us a full share of happiness and prosperity'. However, on New Year's Day itself few GWR staff would have had the chance to spend time in contemplation, as for most it was a normal working day, 1 January not becoming an official bank holiday in England and Wales until 1974. No doubt some employees would have nursed hangovers following the celebrations of the night before, and work would probably have progressed rather more slowly than normal at stations, depots and workshops.

1930

GREETINGS.

On behalf of the Directors and Officers of the Company, I desire to wish all members of the Staff a happy and prosperous New Year.

General Manager

Paddington Station.

For the management of the railway the beginning of a new year was a time to take stock; in the years between the two world wars the Great Western endured some difficult times, and the New Year messages provided by the General Manager to the workforce in the January issue of the company magazine were usually a barometer of the fortunes of the railway and an indication of the issues that then preoccupied both management and staff. The New Year message was also an opportunity to thank staff and encourage greater effort in the coming months, especially in times of difficulty. As early as 1920 Charles Aldington was urging employees to greater efforts, praising their 'fidelity and *esprit de corps*' in the exacting conditions that prevailed in the aftermath of the war. His successor, Felix Pole, continued in this vein four years later, asking staff to go forward with 'every hope' certain of accomplishing much for the benefit of what he called the 'great triple alliance' of GWR staff, customers and shareholders.

In addition to messages of encouragement from the General Manager the January issue of the *Great Western Railway Magazine* usually featured a summary of the past year's achievements, the work of each of the company's principal departments being described in some detail. By the 1930s these articles often ran to more than 25 pages, including descriptions of new work and some statistical and financial highlights. While it is not necessary to offer such a level of detail at this point, a description of the railway and its main activities will provide useful context to the activities chronicled later in the book.

By the 1930s the GWR could boast that it had more than 9,000 miles of track over which its train services ran, describing its territory as being 'roughly defined as within a triangle bounded by lines connecting London and Penzance, Penzance and Liverpool and Liverpool and London'. The railway had expanded

LEFT The General Manager's New Year Message from the January 1930 issue of the *Great Western Railway Magazine*.

TOP RIGHT Crowded platforms at Paddington in the 1920s. It is almost 10.30am, and the 'Cornish Riviera Limited' express is about to depart Platform 1, although there seem to be a large number of passengers yet to get on the train.

BOTTOM RIGHT Paddington seems a world away in this charming view of Porthcawl station in the 1950s. *STEAM/Westrail Enterprises*

PLATFORM Nº1
Nº2 PLATFORM Nº3
TELEGRAPH OFFICE
STATION MASTERS OFFICE
CLOAK ROOM

& WAITING ROOM
STATION MASTER
PARCELS OFFICE AND CLOAK ROOM
Guernsey
BR (W)

LEFT 'Star' 4-6-0 No 4056 *Princess Margaret* heads the up 'Cornish Riviera Limited' past Dawlish in July 1922.

TOP RIGHT A 1930 scene featuring the headquarters of the enlarged GWR Docks Department, established at Cardiff Docks in what prior to the Grouping had been the offices of the Cardiff Railway.

BOTTOM RIGHT An August 1929 view of the *St Julien*, its decks crowded with holidaymakers. GWR ships were used for pleasure trips as well as cross-Channel ferry services, and such may well have been the case here.

significantly following the Grouping process in 1923 and had been the only one of the existing companies to maintain its independence and identity. Pre-Grouping company publicity had styled the GWR as the 'Line of a Thousand Stations', but with the absorption of other railways this figure had grown to 1,623 by 1930. Statistics provided in an introduction to one of its own publications in 1938 reveal that the company was indeed a massive undertaking; in the previous year the GWR had carried some 116 million passengers, along with more than 56 million tons of merchandise and mineral traffic and nearly 1.5 million head of livestock. To handle all this traffic the company employed more than 100,000 staff and owned 3,633 locomotives, 9,021 passenger vehicles and a staggering 93,226 goods wagons.

Although the Great Western is remembered primarily for the glamourous express passenger trains run between the wars, the company's freight business was what enabled it to pay shareholders a dividend every year between 1919 and 1939. Freight, especially the movement of coal, along with the docks owned and directly served by the railway, gave the GWR a steady if sometimes fluctuating income, despite the effects of the General Strike and the Great Depression. The company was fortunate that the area served by its lines included the coalfields of South and North Wales, the Forest of Dean, South Staffordshire and Somerset; in addition, at the Grouping it acquired railways running through some of the most heavily industrialised parts of South Wales, where iron, steel and tinplate production and copper and lead smelting and other manufacturing took place. The reach of the GWR also extended well into the manufacturing heart of the West Midlands and the Black Country, and the railway even catered for traffic in the Liverpool area and to and from the Manchester Ship Canal's docks and the Trafford Park Estate in Manchester, deep in the heart of its rivals' territory.

Through the Grouping the GWR had become one of the largest dock owners in the world, and in addition to the docks and harbours it already owned or operated at Fishguard, Plymouth and Weymouth it had acquired significant operations at Cardiff, Newport, Swansea and a number of other locations in South Wales that were to provide it with significant income, besides having operational implications. In January 1938 the report for the previous year's docks traffic noted that the total tonnage handled by the GWR at its six largest ports (Cardiff, Swansea, Newport, Barry, Port Talbot and Penarth) exceeded 24 million, an increase of 4 million tons over the previous year. Whilst almost every kind of merchandise was handled, the export of coal predominated, although exports of iron and steel, tinplate were also significant. Vast quantities of other goods were imported through the docks, these including oil, manufactured steel, timber and fresh and tinned food. In the winter months citrus fruits were imported from Palestine, and in 1937 more than 200,000 cases of oranges, lemons and grapefruit were landed at Cardiff Docks. Of the other ports managed by the GWR, Plymouth remained significant throughout the 1920s and 1930s as the first port of call for ocean liners discharging mail and passengers. The dock was also the destination for fruit and vegetables imported from the Continent, as was the Dorset port of Weymouth, which handled thousands of tons of fruit, vegetables and flowers from the Channel Islands.

'The Great Western Railway has made cheapness, rapidity and convenience in freight transportation its specialized study,' noted a company booklet in 1936; the goods trains that it ran around the network were supported by a large department which operated goods depots and warehouses of all shapes and sizes, many of which by the late 1930s were provided with modern mechanical cranes and other equipment to handle the huge range of goods being transported. The railway had always offered 'door-to-door' collection and delivery, which before the Great War had been largely still handled by horse-drawn wagons. By 1937 there were more than 5,000 road vehicles in the GWR fleet, and the number of horses used by the railway had dropped to around 1,500.

As road competition made increasing inroads into its freight business the GWR moved into new areas of business which would have seemed unthinkable two decades earlier; it offered and sold warehouse space at its depots to customers, ran a road distribution service to customers in urban areas and set up an extensive

ICE FACTORY
CF 9

ABOVE The large GWR goods depot at Hockley, Birmingham, pictured in 1929.

network of 'Country Lorry Services' to provide deliver agricultural equipment, feed and fertilisers to isolated rural locations. It also developed road-rail containers that could be used both to handle bulk freight loads and as part of a household removal service for domestic customers.

The increasing number of motor vehicles on British roads in the years before World War 2 provided considerable challenges for the GWR, not least in maintaining its passenger-train business, in terms of express passenger services and also slower cross-country and branch-line trains. Although car ownership grew significantly, railway travel was still predominant. The company had 'always had a favourable reputation with travellers', it noted in 1929, its carriages were 'well appointed', and because the line was kept in 'splendid order' trains had 'that smoothness of motion for which the line has been distinguished throughout its history'.

The company could rightly boast about its high-speed long-distance expresses; it could also argue that for almost a quarter of a century its premier service, the 'Cornish Riviera Limited', was 'the longest daily "non-stop" train running in the world', although this distinction was ultimately lost to the LNER in the 1930s. But, the company noted, 'by reason of its luxurious

BELOW For delivering parcels and smaller items the GWR maintained a large fleet of vans, purchased from a number of different manufacturers. This unusual vehicle was built by the Trojan company.

appointments, speed and punctuality' it was still the 'most popular train in the Great Western Railway time-table'. The 'Limited' and other high-speed services like the 'Cheltenham Flyer' were just the pinnacle of summer and winter passenger timetables operated by the Traffic Department that included many fast trains as well as more humble cross-country and local services. Added to these were the many special and excursion trains run by the company in the course of a year. The scale of this traffic was impressive; as an example, in 1936 more than 100,000 people were taken to Windsor for a tour of the castle and a steamer trip of the River Thames. Another 6,000 were transported on 17 trains to visit the new Cunard liner *Queen Mary*, other destinations for excursions that year including London Zoo, Portsmouth Dockyard for a tour of HMS *Victory* and even excursions to the company's own workshops at Swindon. Added to all this were day and evening trips to holiday resorts and to sporting, musical and educational events, all of which combined to generate further revenue for the railway.

None of the work done by the Traffic or Goods departments could operate without the support of other departments tasked with maintaining the railway's infrastructure, signalling, motive power and rolling stock. The Engineering Department was responsible for one of the most important jobs on the railway, the maintenance of the track; in a typical year this might well involve the replacement of more than 300 miles of rail, sleepers and track chairs as well as the day-to-day repair of the permanent way and the bridges, cuttings, embankments and tunnels that made up the railway infrastructure. The department also had responsibility for the maintenance of the GWR estate, which included stations, offices, goods facilities and the docks.

In the 1930s funds made available under the provisions of the Development (Loans & Guarantee) Act 1929 provided support for investment worth millions of pounds and enabled the company to undertake major modernisation schemes at locations such as Paddington, Bristol, Cardiff and Taunton as well as other, smaller projects managed by the Engineering Department all over the network. A good number of these schemes involved improvements to signalling and safety equipment maintained by the Signal Department. Based at its own works at Reading, the department was responsible for not only the hundreds of signalboxes, signals and other safety equipment on the network but also for the telegraph poles and wires linking them. The use of telephones for both business and domestic use increased dramatically in the 1920s and 1930s, and as a result the Signal Department managed and installed new telephone systems in all the major stations and depots as well as providing facilities in other locations such as hotels and refreshment rooms. The department was also responsible for the installation of public-address systems at large stations such as Birmingham Snow Hill and Cardiff as well as electric clocks, which by 1938 numbered in excess of 800. The works at Reading also maintained the old mechanical clocks still in use at smaller

ABOVE A view of the 'Kiddies' Express' run by the GWR from Paddington to Weston-super-Mare on 29 May 1939. As well as the entertainers seen here the train boasted two 'little theatres' and a 'puzzle corner' for younger travellers.

stations and depots all over the network; in 1936 it repaired almost 2,000 clocks and 4,259 watches used by GWR staff.

Of all the departments on the railway, the Chief Mechanical Engineer's Department was arguably one of the most important. With a considerable budget, it was accountable for the design, construction and maintenance of the company's fleet of locomotives, carriages and other rolling stock, as well as the running and manning of the locomotive sheds and depots all over the network. The post of Chief Mechanical Engineer therefore carried a huge responsibility, for not only did he manage the construction and maintenance of the large fleet of locomotives and rolling stock used by the railway; he had also to ensure that it was ready for use by the Traffic Department when required.

The CME's Department was based within the large factory complex at Swindon, where almost all the working equipment used by the railway, from locomotives to lamps, was manufactured. In the interwar years more than 12,000 people were employed there, although the downturn in trade caused by the Depression

ABOVE Passengers are in short supply as diesel railcar No W7 awaits departure from Chipping Norton. Although the photograph was taken in June 1957, little appears to have changed since GWR days.

LEFT A striking view of 'Castle' 4-6-0 No 4076 *Carmarthen Castle*, built at Swindon in February 1924.

led to some redundancies. In its survey for 1937 the GWR noted the work of the department; that year it had built or rebuilt 150 locomotives as well as scrapping 105, some of the latter having been inherited from companies absorbed at the Grouping, others survivors from earlier times, notably the last two 'Barnum' 2-4-0s, built at Swindon as early as 1889. In the Carriage & Wagon Works 478 new carriages had been built, this total including 290 new standard main-line coaches, 150 horseboxes and 12 milk-tank trucks. More than 5,500 wagons were built the previous year, a record, with standard open wagons predominating. Other work undertaken by the department included the construction of containers, road vehicles and the installation of electric power in various depots and docks. Another important role was the running of locomotive sheds and depots; maintaining locomotives at sheds was vitally important, and an army of fitters, cleaners, steam-raisers and boilersmiths supported the large complement of drivers and firemen who operated the locomotives.

The train services run by the GWR were augmented by various other forms of transport; in addition to the fleet of lorries it used to support its freight business, until 1928 it owned a large number of buses used to provide services to areas not served directly by its lines, or to carry passengers on excursions or tours. An agreement with a number of large bus companies such as Crosville, Devon General and Western National led to partnerships' being formed to run services and a withdrawal by the GWR from direct involvement in bus operation. While inevitably meaning a loss of direct control for the railway the arrangement seems to have worked well and reduced unnecessary competition. By 1938 the GWR was able to report that the joint working arrangements had 'become a matter of every-day routine' and that an interesting development had been the 'interchange of omnibus and railway tickets', which had proved 'a great convenience to passengers'.

The railway's maritime interests extended further than the ownership and operation of its docks and harbours; it also ran a steamship fleet that provided services from Fishguard to Rosslare and Waterford and from Weymouth to the Channel Islands. Considerable investment in the 1920s and 1930s saw many of the aged ships used on these services replaced by larger and more modern vessels. The Channel Islands operation, as well as providing a regular passenger service, especially during the summer months, also provided substantial income through the transportation of

ABOVE **Although it purchased some goods and services from outside suppliers the GWR was largely self-sufficient, producing 'in-house' much of what it needed to operate. This photograph shows the ticket-printing facility at Paddington.**

early-season fruit and vegetables from Jersey and Guernsey. In the summer steamers were also used extensively on excursion trips from Weymouth, Plymouth, Torquay and Dartmouth; at the last-mentioned location the GWR also operated a ferry service across the River Dart, providing a link with Kingswear.

In the 1930s the GWR operated limited air services to augment its passenger-train timetable. Scheduled flights began in April 1933 on a route linking Cardiff, Haldon Aerodrome (near Teignmouth) and Plymouth. The following year the 'Big Four' railways set up the Railway Air Services Co. in conjunction with Imperial Airways, using larger aircraft and operating more routes. By 1937 the company was able to report that services were operating on weekdays between Liverpool and Brighton, calling at Birmingham, Cheltenham, Bristol and Ryde, and between Bristol and Plymouth, calling at Cardiff and Exeter. With relatively small passenger capacities and high fares, the services were never profitable but nevertheless provided the railway with some useful publicity.

There is little doubt that the work done by the GWR in advertising and publicising its activities in the years before World War 2 made a huge impact both in raising its profile and in generating revenue for the company. Felix Pole, appointed General Manager in 1921, was a strong advocate of increased commercial advertising of all sorts and making use of all manner of opportunities to publicise the work and services of the railway. As a result its profile was maintained through press stories, issued on a regular basis, that included the inauguration of new activities such as the railway air services, and also new locomotives, rolling stock and trains. The GWR also worked intensively with local councils and resort operators before and during the summer season to increase trade and interest in the holiday resorts served by its trains.

Much of the material issued by the railway was printed in house; in 1937 it was reported that it had produced more than 80 tons of folders, pamphlets, letterpress posters and handbills for

ABOVE The GWR was still using horses for shunting in the 1950s, when this photograph was taken, but the relevance of the scene is unclear; a handwritten caption on the back of the print notes that it was sent to the Dorman Long engineering company.

issue to the public, while the twice-yearly GWR public timetables sold at 6d a copy had amounted to more than 55 tons of paper. The company also produced its own tickets for use at stations, often printing more than 80 million of these annually. Other, more elaborate publicity material was produced externally, including its pictorial posters, jigsaw puzzles and books. In 1936 alone the railway introduced 36 new poster designs, many produced by the best poster artists of the time. *Holiday Haunts*, its premier publication for advertising holiday resorts, accommodation and information about its services, grew both in size and sales during the interwar period; by 1935 it had grown to more than 1,000 pages and was selling in excess of 160,000 copies.

Marketing itself as the 'Holiday Line', the GWR, not surprisingly, was also directly involved in the holiday business itself, both through the train services it ran to resorts and in the management of a number of hotels. The Hotels & Refreshment Rooms Department was responsible for four hotels, the largest of which was the Great Western Royal Hotel at Paddington. This impressive facility, which by the 1930s had become something of an anachronism, was by the end of the decade completely refurbished, complementing modernisation work undertaken the station nearby. The Fishguard Bay Hotel similarly was of a rather old-fashioned nature; its remote location and the gradual decline of the port as a major destination for anything other than the scheduled ferry crossings between Fishguard and Southern Ireland meant that major investment was targeted elsewhere. In addition the company owned two hotels in the West of England, these being the Tregenna Castle Hotel at St Ives and the Manor House Hotel at Moretonhampstead in Devon.

Besides hotels the department was responsible for the vast array of refreshment rooms to be found at stations all over the network; these varied enormously in size and in the range of fare offered, but many were modernised in the 1920s and 1930s. This

GWR

HOLIDAY RETURN TICKETS

TO

IRELAND

JANUARY 1st
and until further notice

TICKETS WILL BE ISSUED ON THE DAYS SPECIFIED HEREUNDER, AVAILABLE BY ORDINARY SERVICES IN EACH DIRECTION AND FOR RETURN ON ANY SAILING DATE UP TO AND INCLUDING THE MONDAY FORTNIGHT FROM DATE OF ISSUE (WHERE SERVICE PERMITS):—

Fridays and Saturdays ..	.. Via Fishguard and Rosslare
Fridays and Saturdays ..	.. Via Liverpool and Dublin; B. & I. S.P. Co.
Fridays and Saturdays ..	.. Via Liverpool and Belfast SS. Co.
Fridays, Saturdays and Sundays ..	Via Heysham and Belfast.
Fridays, Saturdays and Sundays ..	Via Holyhead and Kingstown.
Thursdays and Saturdays ..	.. Via Fishguard and City of Cork S.P. Co.
Fridays	.. Via Fishguard and Waterford Direct Boat.

TICKETS ISSUED AND DATED IN ADVANCE AT ALL STATIONS, TOWN OFFICES AND AGENCIES

GENERAL NOTICES AND CONDITIONS OF ISSUE OF HOLIDAY RETURN TICKETS.

Holiday Return Tickets are issued at less than the ordinary fares and are subject to the notices and conditions shewn in the Company's time tables.

Children under three years of age, Free; three and under fourteen, Half-price, except via Liverpool (Landing Stage), which will be half adult fare, plus 2d.

Passengers holding Holiday Return Tickets are allowed free conveyance of personal luggage, not exceeding in weight 150 lbs. (First Class) or 100 lbs. (Third Class).

Arrangements will be made for the issue of Holiday Return Tickets from any station not shewn herein upon prior notice being given at the station from which the journey will be commenced.

For any further information, application should be made at any of the Company's Stations, Town Offices or Agencies; or to Mr. H. L. Wilkinson, Superintendent of the Line, Paddington Station, London, W.2.

Paddington Station,
January, 1935.

JAMES MILNE,
General Manager.

investment was justified as revenues steadily improved; 'efforts to maintain the highest standards and improved values to the travelling public,' it was argued, 'had been reflected in increased receipts'. The income generated by refreshment rooms was augmented by restaurant and buffet cars on many of the most important expresses. The complex work of preparing and serving high-quality fare in such cramped surroundings was a source of pride for the company, and in the years before World War 2 investment in new rolling stock ensured that standards could be maintained.

Needless to say, the work of the GWR extended well beyond the departments to which reference is made above, and further details of some of the activities mentioned appear later in the book; the purpose of this introduction had been to provide some context to the many seasonal activities described elsewhere and hopefully lend a sense of scale to an operation that employed so many staff and did so much over the course of a year.

ABOVE LEFT **A GWR handbill advertising excursion tickets for Ireland, travel being on its own services from Fishguard and on LMS ferries from further north.**

ABOVE RIGHT **The cover of a publicity booklet issued by the GWR in 1929.**

RIGHT **The loading of cars onto ferries was rather more complicated than it is today, as is apparent from this photograph taken at Fishguard Harbour in May 1937.**

PART 1: WINTER

'A long railway journey in the winter is much more interesting than many people might imagine,' asserted W. H. Owens, writing in the *Great Western Railway Magazine* in 1935. Unless they were regular commuters, many passengers using 'Gods Wonderful Railway' might well travel significant distances only during the holiday season and, the writer continued, would consider a journey in the winter months 'a cold and uncomfortable business'. However, the passenger on a GWR train at that time of year would probably see a landscape that was rather more varied than might first be expected; winter sunshine, Owens noted, gave 'beauty to the dullest objects', and at the end of the day the sunset gave leafless trees 'a rare charm'. The GWR staff charged with keeping the railway running in winter might well have taken issue with this rather idyllic description, especially as Owens concluded his article by arguing that 'until you have made a journey to the West in the coldest weather, you may never fully realise the winter comforts of a railway compartment'. Staff working out on the line in such conditions would surely have seen things rather differently.

W. H. Owens also remarked that travelling across England through a snow-covered landscape had been one of his happiest railway memories; to appreciate the real beauty of snow, he wrote, 'you must see it lying on the hillsides and meadows. Is there anything to compare with a railway train for this purpose?' The ability of railways to cope with difficult winter weather was due in no small part to their workforce, who worked

BELOW The Princetown branch, on Dartmoor, was usually badly affected by snow. This 1891 view features an unidentified GWR tank engine and a single carriage stuck in a snowdrift.

ABOVE **A wintry scene at Paddington, this being the view west from Bishop's Road Bridge.**

long hours to keep the network running. Although the GWR was generally less affected by snow than were some of the other 'Big Four' companies its staff still struggled to keep the network running in winter, especially on routes which crossed high ground. A number of the Welsh railways absorbed in 1923 had lines that could be badly affected by snow, especially in the South Wales valleys and on the old Cambrian lines. Even routes in the West of England were not immune; the 10-mile branch line from Yelverton to Princetown climbed almost 1,400ft to the terminus serving Dartmoor Prison and was a particularly bleak route. When snow fell on Dartmoor the line was usually affected; in March 1891, following very severe weather in the West of England, a train from Princetown with six passengers on board was stranded for two nights in a snow-filled cutting, and conditions on the line were so bad that it did not fully reopen for almost a week.

Entitled 'Where the Railways beat the Roads', the editorial to the *Railway Gazette* for January 1928 reported that the reliability of railways in adverse weather had been in sharp contrast to 'modern motor traffic', which had been 'hopelessly beaten' by the severe winter conditions which that year had made large areas of the country 'largely impassable' at times. Snow and frost had ruled out motor travel as a reliable means of maintaining travel and food supplies, the piece continued, noting that many long-distance coach operators which had boasted that they would soon replace railway services were forced to cancel their own services, with the result passengers who had booked to travel from Cheltenham to Oxford by coach had instead to complete their journey by GWR train. Whilst the *Railway Gazette* could not be blamed for seizing the opportunity to take a swipe at what it saw as the growing menace of road competition, the article contained more than a little hubris from an industry that for most of the year was finding it increasingly difficult to compete with the bus, the car and the lorry.

The conditions experienced by the railway between the two world wars, while at times difficult, were eclipsed by the arctic conditions that gripped Britain in 1947 when, as Adrian Vaughan noted, an already cold winter 'exploded into a blizzard of legendary proportions'. While the situation in the London Division was not ideal, further west matters were far worse; locomotives, points, signals and water troughs froze solid, and railway staff struggled to get to work. In the South Wales valleys, it was reported, more than 200 collieries were snowed in, and wagons full of coal were buried under drifts. Although the snow eased off on 3 February the respite was brief, and within a few days the blizzards began again, accompanied by sub-zero temperatures. The Plymouth Division was particularly badly affected, and Adrian Vaughan also records that snowdrifts were so deep that staff from Laira shed looking for the snowplough kept at Tavistock Junction had great difficulty in locating it, as it was buried under a smooth blanket of snow.

As had been the case in 1891 the Princetown branch was once again blocked; a train sent from Yelverton to clear the line on 31 January 1947 battled its way through drifts that were up to 14ft high, reaching Princetown after a four-hour journey that had seen one steam locomotive fail. The return journey became even more eventful when the train became stuck in a large snowdrift, stranding the gang of men sent to accompany the train crew. The train was eventually rescued, but the line was not fully reopened until 3 February. The severe weather did not abate until March, when the thaw caused further damage through flooding and landslips on the Great Western network. The extreme weather conditions experienced by staff and public alike in 1946 and 1947 were far more serious and prolonged than anything experienced in the years between the two world wars but serve to illustrate just how resilient the railway and its people were.

When snow fell heavily in areas served by the GWR, snowploughs retained at most major locomotive sheds, like the one used on the Princetown branch, were naturally brought into action to clear main lines first and then branches. When weather was very severe however, staff were called out to shift snowdrifts

BELOW The winter of 1946/7 brought arctic conditions not seen in Britain for generations. Just how heavy the snow was in South Wales is illustrated by the size of the drift through which this pannier tank and an unidentified second locomotive are picking their way with an inspection saloon.

by hand; as Vaughan noted, in very bad conditions passenger trains were kept running only by calling out every permanent-way man on the main line and branches to keep points clear of snow. High winds blew snow across running lines and into point work, causing it to jam; when snow and ice was jammed into crossings and points it could also then derail locomotives and rolling stock, causing further disruption. An additional problem encountered in wintry conditions was that of telegraph wires being brought down by the weight of snow that had settled on them, something GWR staff were powerless to prevent; when this occurred the block-telegraph communication system between signalboxes was put out of action, and train services were suspended for safety reasons. The impact of such events could be far-reaching and ultimately expensive for the company; a northeasterly blizzard on the night of 27 February 1937 was so severe on lines between Carmarthen and Aberystwyth and Borth and Aberdovey that the Signal Department was forced to provide more than 100 telegraph poles and 800 miles of new wire to make good the damage.

ABOVE The heavy trains sent to clear the snowdrifts were often double- or even triple-headed. Seen coupled to the front of one such train are a pair of ex-Rhymney Railway 0-6-2Ts, Nos 80 and 81, and an unidentified 0-6-0 tender engine.

Heavy snow settling on signals and signalling equipment could also cause severe difficulties; in the years prior to World War 1 there had been a number of accidents on other railways as a result of snow either obstructing drivers' view of signals or preventing signal arms from returning to Danger. As a consequence instructions were issued to employees in October 1923 to the effect that in snowy or frosty conditions a member of track or signal staff must 'see that nothing interferes with the true working of the Arms or Discs, and Lamps of the Signals' and that 'Signal Arms, Lamp Glasses and Spectacles are kept clear from snow'. The instructions also required staff to check signal wires and pulleys to ensure they were working freely and not jammed by snow.

In periods of prolonged cold weather staff also struggled to cope as locomotive water cranes, tanks and pipes froze; many

ABOVE **To prevent its pipe from freezing in winter the water crane at Hemyock, Devon, was equipped with a coal brazier complete with a tall chimney.**

water cranes were provided with coal-fired braziers to prevent this, but not all equipment could be thus protected. On station platforms fire buckets and other water containers needed special care in winter weather, and each year stationmasters were instructed to ensure that 'fire buckets, dip tanks or tubs, which normally contain water, are to be kept clear of ice during frost'. Buckets 'should be placed in sheltered or warm positions' where practicable, a circular noted, or, if this were not possible, they should be emptied and placed near a fire hydrant instead. These instructions were issued, it was noted in 1930, to prevent a recurrence of a situation that had arisen the previous year, when 'a large number of buckets which had been damaged by bursting had to be returned to Swindon for repairs', causing 'considerable expense'. Even though steam locomotives had fireboxes full of hot coals, pipework, hand tools and even the coal in their tenders froze in very severe weather; the arctic conditions experienced in 1947 led to piles of coal being burned in shed sidings in an attempt to prevent locomotives from freezing up.

Between the two world wars snow and prolonged cold weather were, fortunately, only rarely the cause of severe delays and disruption, but the same could not be said of fog. Warm, moist air, combined with the cold ground, a lack of wind and the effects of thousands of coal fires, was perfect for creating 'pea soup' winter fog, a potentially dangerous and disruptive situation for the GWR. Some idea of the impact of the fog can be gained from the example of just one year, 1929. Adrian Vaughan records that dense fog was experienced on the network on 21, 22 and 23 January, 6 February, 26 and 27 February and for a prolonged period between 18 and 27 March. Matters were not helped by further fog on 8 April and unseasonal heavy snow four days later. There was further fog in November, ending a difficult year for the railway. An article in the *Bristol Times & Mirror* newspaper of 11 December the following year reported that 'widespread fog over the South of England was responsible for the slowing down of traffic' but that local train services were subject to only 'minor delays'. By far the worst conditions, however, were usually experienced in the Thames Valley, which, as B. E. Pugh noted in an article published more than 60 years later, was notorious for 'pea-soup fogs that could descend with frightening rapidity and blanket scores of square miles in no time at all'. Special arrangements and contingency plans were therefore kept in place to ensure that a limited train service could be operated safely in foggy conditions.

Company instructions issued by the Superintendent of the Line in September 1929 regarding 'Through Trains to and from London when Fog prevails in the London Division' reveal a much-reduced seven-page timetable that contained a large number of cancelled services and revised working arrangements largely for afternoon and overnight trains. Not surprisingly, the use of slip coaches was suspended in fog, trains calling at stations instead of having carriages detached. As an example, instructions noted that the 2.10pm Paddington–Birkenhead was 'to call instead of slip at Banbury' but would 'carry usual slip tail signals'. In general through express trains were restricted to eight 70ft or nine 60ft carriages, and services often made additional stops at intermediate stations to make up for other cancelled trains. As journey times were often prolonged or delayed because of the fog the timetable also noted a number of trains where dining cars were to be added to provide sustenance for travellers; staff were reminded that, in the case of trains working without advertised restaurant cars, passengers 'must be specially canvassed' to encourage them to purchase lunch and tea baskets for their journey.

Special arrangements were also put in place to ensure that milk traffic was dealt with promptly. Milk vans were not, however,

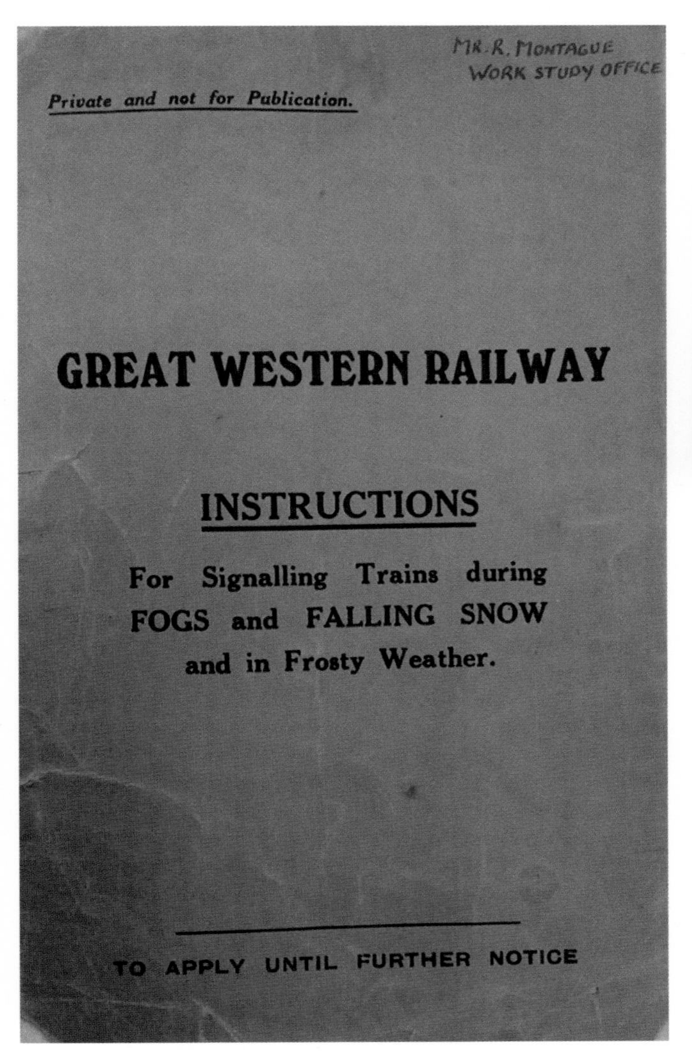
MR. R. MONTAGUE
WORK STUDY OFFICE

Private and not for Publication.

GREAT WESTERN RAILWAY

INSTRUCTIONS

For Signalling Trains during FOGS and FALLING SNOW and in Frosty Weather.

TO APPLY UNTIL FURTHER NOTICE

ABOVE For obvious reasons, few photographs were taken in foggy conditions. This rare and murky image of a BR Standard tank engine was recorded at the ex-GWR station at Leamington Spa in 1950.

LEFT GWR Fog Instructions, 1930.

to be attached to passenger trains, 'with the exception of odd milk churns loaded as usual into the train vans', it was noted. Instead 'Special Milk Trains' were timetabled, among them the 9.0am from Oxford to Paddington, calling at locations on the Wycombe line and stations in West London, and the 2.0pm Swindon–Paddington, which called at larger stations in the Thames Valley and also included milk from connecting trains originating in Bristol and Cheltenham. Not recorded in the 1929 instructions was the fact that normally most goods trains were either terminated or placed in loops up and down the line, to avoid lengthy delays to passenger services. This caused considerable disruption to the operation of freight trains, especially if fog persisted, but running a limited passenger timetable was difficult enough without the added complication of slow-moving coal and goods trains clogging the running lines. Some exceptions to these rules were made, however, notably for long-distance mail, newspapers and perishable goods.

To enable trains to run in foggy conditions special working arrangements were in place, to ensure the safe operation of the kind of limited timetable already described. The decision to institute what was called 'Fog Working' was normally made by Divisional Superintendents following advice from signalmen along the line. Each signalman had a number of 'fog objects' or landmarks that he could see from his signalbox, and as he gradually lost sight of these he would telephone the local control office, enabling a picture of the extent and thickness of the fog to be gathered. If the situation were deemed serious, local stationmasters or signalmen had instructions to call out 'Fogmen', usually permanent-way staff who would act as fog signalmen while visibility was poor. The names of these staff were on a list kept at each 'box or station; if they could not be contacted by telephone a lad porter or signalbox call boy would be sent out to inform them.

Detailed instructions were provided for all involved, including signalmen, stationmasters and fogmen; reporting to a station or signalbox, the fogman was to be supplied with '36 detonators (or more if necessary), a Hand Signal lamp, trimmed and lighted, and a Red and Green Flag'. Each fogman was then deployed at signals to assist train crews in observing them in poor visibility; when a signal was at 'Danger' two detonators were placed on the rail 10 yards apart some way away from the signal itself. The fogman stood close by, his hand lamp showing red, warning approaching trains not to proceed past the signal. If the hand lamp was not seen, the detonators would explode with a loud bang as the train ran over them, providing a very obvious warning to train crews. When a detonator was exploded 'the Engine Driver

ABOVE **The wintry conditions seem appropriate to the sombre occasion as the funeral train of GWR Chairman Viscount Churchill passes through Oxford on 6 January 1936.**

must immediately reduce speed and bring his train under complete control so as to obey any signal,' instructions stated. Once the signal at Danger was lowered, detonators were removed, and the train could proceed; the fogman was also responsible for checking that there were no obstructions such as broken-down trains on the line; if there were any, the instructions noted, he should go back up the line 'a sufficient distance' to protect the obstruction and lay further detonators to warn locomotive crews of the hazard.

Small wooden fogmen's huts were provided at certain distant signals, affording at least some protection from the elements; these also contained a telephone which the fogman could use to inform the signalbox of the safe passing of trains. While providing a good source of overtime in winter months the job of fogman was not an easy option, and the role carried great responsibility; apart from the unpleasant weather, they also needed to remain very alert and aware of possible danger over a prolonged period and as a result, GWR rules noted that fogmen should be relieved after 12 hours' duty. Instructions also required that they should not be kept out on the track for more than six hours if they had begun fogging work after the completion of a normal day's employment on the railway.

An additional safety feature for locomotive crews in fog or snow was the Automatic Train Control (ATC) system; first trialled before the Great War, ATC employed ramps fixed to the permanent way at distant signals which provided a warning bell signal to drivers if the signal was at danger. If the warning was not cancelled the brakes would be activated and the train stopped before reaching the home signal. If the distant signal was clear, the train could proceed; the value of this facility was that it facilitated 'the running of the train when the semaphore signals cannot be seen during fogs and snow-storms', according to W. G. Chapman in the GWR publication *The 10.30 Limited*. Good though the system was, its introduction was slow, and in 1929 it was in use only on the routes from Paddington to Reading, Oxford, Swindon and Wycombe; the following year it was installed on routes to Plymouth, Swansea and Wolverhampton, but its use was never extended to all main-line routes.

The poor conditions suffered by staff working in foggy or snowy weather were exacerbated by the shorter days and dark winter nights. Even in the 1920s electric lighting was not universal in stations, goods depots and other facilities on the railway, and in some cases gas lighting was not replaced until the 1940s. As one correspondent noted in the company magazine, weary clerks working late with 'aching brains' owed 'a heavy debt of gratitude' when electric light was installed for not only was the light under which they worked brighter, they were also not choked by gas fumes. However well-lit facilities were, the long dark nights proved too much of a temptation for some less-honest staff, and in February 1922 it was reported that 'taking advantage, probably, of the long periods of darkness' at that time of year, some of the company's employees at various places on the network had helped themselves to articles in transit on the railway. 'Pilfering on the railway and elsewhere is very prevalent ... and done by men who receive good wages,' it was noted, along with the fact that many railway staff with previously excellent service records were now being sent to prison as a result.

Electric lighting made the work of those working outside in stations, goods yards and engine sheds that much safer, especially where complicated and potentially dangerous shunting took place, although working in such places remained difficult in the darkness of winter conditions. By the 1920s GWR staff were issued with heavy greatcoats to give some protection against the cold, although this had not always been the case; in 1892 men employed on horse-drawn wagons at Paddington were moved to pass a resolution of thanks to the GWR's directors for issuing them with overcoats that winter. Whatever protection staff might be afforded, working on the railway in the winter months was nevertheless tough, and a goods guard reminiscing about his working life summed up the experience: 'Feel the cold? I should think we did!'

While frost, fog and snow provided serious disruption to GWR services on a number of occasions between the wars, a rather more consistent problem faced by the railway in winter was rain, heavy downpours often causing difficulties and delays in terms of flooding and of landslips in cuttings and embankments. Flood water damaged the track formation, washing away ballast and earthworks and, where it was more than several feet deep, prevented the passage of trains by extinguishing locomotive fires.

BELOW Flooding was not confined to permanent way and stations, as illustrated by this March 1922 photograph taken inside the Blaen Rhondda Tunnel.

4986

LEFT **Newly built 'Hall' 4-6-0 No 4986 *Aston Hall* poses for the camera at Swindon Works on 26 January 1931. The photograph was taken to illustrate the fitting of Automatic Train Control equipment to the GWR locomotive fleet.**

RIGHT **One of a series taken by the GWR for use in a catalogue of staff uniforms, this photograph illustrates one of the heavy greatcoats used by yard staff and draymen.**

The Meteorological Office monthly report for January 1925 notes that the high winds and rain that had begun after Christmas in 1924 continued into the first few days of the new year. The result of the gales and rain were reported by the Divisional Superintendent at Bristol on 3 January, when he recorded that single-line working had been required on more than four miles of the Great Western main line from Steventon to Wantage Road as a result of a slip, causing 'serious delay' to traffic. There was also flooding at Dauntsey, near Wootton Bassett, requiring the up and down distant signals to be held at Danger to warn footplate staff of the flood water on the line. Staff were requested to monitor the situation closely, as the resulting delays from these signal checks were of great concern to management. At the same time serious flooding was reported on the Bristol & South Wales Direct line at Chipping Sodbury, resulting from water coming out of the tunnel there. Almost three miles in length, the tunnel provided the GWR with an ongoing problem, as its bore, which had been excavated through an outlier of the Cotswolds, cut through a number of springs. When these became swollen by winter rain, the tunnel tended to flood on a regular basis, often closing the line completely. On this occasion in 1925 a locomotive was stationed at Chipping Sodbury to provide assistance to trains if required, presumably due to the amount of flood water still present. The tunnel has continued to suffer from flooding, even in more recent times. In addition to these more serious incidents there were reports of other landslips 'not of a serious character' at locations such as Clifton Bridge, Pill and Flax Bourton.

In January 1928 the *Great Western Railway Magazine* described the consequences of 'A Great Snow Storm' which had blanketed the South of England, West Country and South Wales on Christmas Day and Boxing Day, causing considerable delays to services. Severe gales and storms followed the snow on 1 and 2 January, and the ensuing thaw had severe consequences in the South of England, including an unprecedented tidal surge on the River Thames which caused serious flooding in Central London. The GWR did not escape this bad weather, and the company magazine reported that lines were badly affected by flooding in a number of places including Newbury. Aside from having to reduce speed when passing though flooded areas 'train services were not materially affected,' the article concluded. It also noted, however, that during the 'heavy and wide-spread' snow storm the company's Tregenna Castle Hotel at St Ives was 'entirely immune' from the poor weather, although it did not elaborate as to how snowbound traveller would have reached the west of Cornwall! There were further gales in February of the same year, and on the 13th *The Times* reported on a storm that had caused severe damage, notably bringing down many chimneys and blowing away roofs in the Midlands and the West Country. The poor weather of 1928 had a human as well as financial cost, *The Times* also noting that a GWR platelayer, Evan Watkins, had been killed in an accident as a consequence of bad weather at Brecon; he had been knocked down by a locomotive, the article concluded, as, owing to a terrific gale, he had failed to hear it coming.

The West of England was struck by further stormy weather in 1930. Presaging the events of 2014, a severe gale on the night of 4 January undermined the sea wall at Dawlish, about half a mile east of the station, washing away the promenade and undermining around 50ft of the foundations, leaving the track completely unsupported. The sea wall, built by Brunel as part of the South Devon Railway and extended in the years before the Great War, had always provided the GWR with more than its share of engineering problems and since its construction in the 1840s had been breached a number of times in severe weather. The wall itself was almost ¾ mile long and 45ft wide, built from limestone blocks, behind which was a filling of hard rubble; separating the railway from a public promenade was a parapet wall. Although repair work was begun straightaway, further high tides washed away the repaired section and threatened more of the sea wall. Special gangs of permanent-way staff were then drafted in as a matter of urgency to work night and day, initially to protect and then to rebuild the wall. To reinforce it new granite blocks were lowered into place and secured with quick-setting mortar, following which the large hole behind the sea wall was laboriously filled. With the line completely blocked while work took place, train services were diverted, some using the Teign Valley branch, while the more important expresses, including the 'Cornish Riviera Limited' ran via the Southern Railway route between Exeter and Plymouth. Despite further atrocious weather, work on the sea wall was completed by Wednesday 11 January, and the following day all services were back to normal. In 1935 W. G. Chapman described the sea wall at Dawlish in the company's *Track Topics* publication as being 'most important' to

ABOVE **Damage to the sea wall at Dawlish remains an ongoing problem for the railway. This photograph shows repair work underway on 23 March 1966 after the wall had been breached in heavy storms.**

the railway whilst noting that steps taken by its engineers in constructing groynes and other work had rendered 'attacks by the sea on this stretch of line less effective'.

The appalling conditions continued, and on the night of 12 January 1930 the Bristol Division was hit by a severe gale. Newspapers reported that hundreds of trees had been felled by the high winds across much of England and Wales, and no doubt GWR permanent-way staff spent many hours clearing debris from the track that night and in the days following. Signals and telegraph posts were blown down, and damage was caused to station and goods-shed roofs, although no serious interference to traffic resulted, the Divisional Superintendent noted some weeks later. That damage was kept to a minimum was largely thanks to the work of the permanent-way gangs, who kept the lineside as clear as possible by cutting back trees and shrubs — just one of a number of seasonal tasks carried out in addition to the routine work done by platelayers and gangers. Regular maintenance on the line was divided into 'lengths' looked after by gangs of track staff and overseen by the Length Ganger, who walked his stretch of line daily. He and his gang were responsible for the track, fencing and hedges, drains and keeping lineside vegetation at bay. The track gangs also had to contend with a rather more unusual pest; describing damage to telegraph and fence posts, the *Great Western Railway Magazine* for December 1937 reported 'extensive depredation' on the Tenbury line where it passed through the Wyre Forest, 'a veritable home' to the lesser-spotted woodpecker.

The most important work done by the permanent-way gang was inspecting and repairing the track formation; checks were made to ensure that rails, points or crossings were not damaged or defective and that the track gauge was correct. As rails were not continuously welded together as they are today, one of the most laborious tasks undertaken, winter or summer, was the checking and oiling of the fishplates that joined rail lengths. Edward Hadley, Editor of the *Great Western Railway Magazine*, spent a week working with a gang of platelayers in 1928 as research for an article and described the hard work involved in removing and oiling the fishplates. The oil used was 'a special mixture as black as tar and about as thick as treacle', he reported, adding that, because it stuck to his hands, his face also ended up being covered in oil as he wiped away perspiration. Track staff also kept ballast clean and free from weeds, as well as filling any holes under the sleepers; until the 1930s weedkiller was applied by hand, a highly labour-intensive task requiring numerous watering cans, but the introduction of regular weed-killing trains that sprayed the track with sodium chlorate made this work rather easier; however, to minimise the hazard to passengers and staff the machines were not used at stations or in goods yards.

Permanent-way gangs began work early, starting their shift at 7am; in the winter it was usually dark when men came on duty, and, not surprisingly, the shorter days restricted the amount of work that could be done. Staff huts or cabins built at regular intervals along the line were not only used to store tools and materials but also provided shelter from the elements, where men could rest and take meal breaks. In his 1928 article Edward Hadley described how it was normal practice for men to bring the raw materials (in his case several rashers of bacon and an egg) to be cooked by one of the gang ready for breakfast at 8.30am. As well as a half-hour break for breakfast the men were allowed 45 minutes for dinner at 1pm but thereafter continued until 5pm, which made their shift a long and difficult one, especially in hostile winter weather.

The magazine article describes the physical effort required by platelayers to ensure that the line was kept in perfect condition; the painstaking and sometimes backbreaking work required of track staff was assisted by the introduction of more mechanical equipment in the 1930s, but much of the work remained very labour-intensive, and gangs continued to look after their track lengths with pride until well after World War 2. This obvious pride in the job was fostered by the company, which promoted a regular annual competition to find the best track length gang on the system. Awards were presented to the gangs 'whose length was maintained at the highest standard of efficiency', the *Great Western Railway Magazine* reported in August 1938, naming 11 permanent-way gangs — one from each division — as winners that year. They represented a real cross-section of the railway, from locations as diverse as Cheltenham, Dauntsey, Ferndale,

BELOW A permanent-way gang hard at work at Bristol Temple Meads on 30 August 1930. In the background can be seen the old carriage shed, destined to be swept away in the modernisation of the station.

Gerrards Cross, St Clears and Talyllyn. Despite the important role played by track staff in ensuring that trains ran safely, it was noted that gangers were conscious that, as a group, they were not held in great esteem; 'because of his hob-nailed boots, and dust-laden and oil-soaked clothes, he receives sparse consideration and scant respect,' the magazine article concluded.

Besides the physical effort needed to work on the track, gangers also faced greater hazards than did most other workers on the Great Western. In the 1920s it was noted that every year there were on Britain's railways more than 3,000 accidents involving track staff, more than 70 losing their lives. Casualties were not uncommon on the GWR; two serious accidents in 1921 and 1922 showing just how dangerous it was for permanent-way staff. On 26 September 1921 a ganger and four of his team were killed by a passenger train at Stapleton Road station in Bristol, while seven months later, on 24 March 1922, an 'under-ganger' and three others were killed by a light-engine at Wilmcote. These casualties and many other injuries were in spite of considerable work already done by all the railways to try to engender a safety culture amongst their staff; the GWR had been the first company

ABOVE Cement being pumped behind the walls of the Severn Tunnel in the early 1930s, the work being undertaken by the GWR in conjunction with the Cementation Co. The dirty clothes of the men hard at work contrast markedly with the clean suits of management on the left.

to run a safety campaign for its employees, and in 1914 it published a 48-page booklet, 'The Safety Movement', based on a series of articles presented the year before in the company magazine. The book was wide-ranging, covering all aspects of railway operation, including the use of equipment within workshops like those at Swindon, as well as information aimed at track, station and locomotive staff.

Accidents involving permanent-way staff continued to be a concern for GWR management after the Great War, and in a 1928 article in the company magazine it was noted that its editor, Edward Hadley, had written a new book, *Accident Prevention for Permanent Way Men*, copies of which had been circulated to every one of its permanent-way staff — 12,000 men in all. The article provided some highlights from the new book, which, with 'a profusion of illustrations', demonstrated some of the safety messages being put forward by the company. Close attention was paid to the hazards of working on and crossing the line, loading and lifting, the safe use of tools and equipment, and the subject of practical jokes. 'Many a prank, intended "just for fun", has lost a man a limb, his sight or his life,' the article noted.

Throughout the 1920s and 1930s the company used other techniques to reinforce the safety message, and in addition to regular reports and articles in the company magazine it inaugurated a 'Freedom from Accident' campaign, which took the form of a competition with GWR staff organised into teams, which gained points for each month of the year they avoided injury. Weekly instructions issued to staff by the Superintendent of the Line also made reference to safety issues from time to time; one such warning appeared in February 1930, when it was noted that there had been 'a serious increase in the number of articles ... found on the line, having fallen off in transit'. Employees were reminded of the importance of ensuring that all traffic in wagons was secured, not only to reduce compensation claims from consignees but also to prevent track staff from being injured or killed.

Safety for track-maintenance staff remained a matter of great importance for the Great Western, and in 1936 it issued another booklet, titled *Look Out! Some Hints for Permanent-Way Men*. Its introduction began: 'Personal Safety may not be a popular phrase with you, and often may not seem to fit in with the initiative your job demands.' The new booklet reinforced the familiar safety messages contained in earlier publications and rulebooks but also highlighted new hazards now facing permanent-way staff, illustrated by coloured line drawings instead of photographs. These new threats included the danger posed by the introduction some years earlier of diesel railcars; these vehicles differed from steam locomotives in a number of important respects, the book recorded, most notably their 'quiet approach at all speed' and the fact that there was 'little vibration on the rails'. Extra vigilance was required in areas where railcars were in operation, staff were reminded, with an illustration of a railcar titled 'the Unheard Train' to reinforce the message. Staff were also alerted to the dangers of working on electrified lines, something not mentioned in previous booklets. Although this form of traction was 'at present confined to the London Division' it called for 'special precautions by the permanent way staff', the book concluded. Employees were warned not to cross live rails unless absolutely necessary, and as rubber was a 'non-conductor' every man was required to have a pair of rubber gauntlets with him while on duty.

Safety was of paramount importance for permanent-way and engineering staff working at one of the most important locations on the GWR network away from large centres like Paddington and Swindon. By the interwar period the Severn Tunnel — the construction of which was described by one GWR writer as 'the result of thirteen years' fight by indomitable engineers and their staff' — was more than 30 years old and in need of some major maintenance. To reduce disruption and delay to train services on

ABOVE A dark winter's evening at Paddington in the 1950s.

BELOW The main pump-house for the Severn Tunnel at Sudbrook. Inside were six 70in Cornish beam-engines capable of pumping 25 million gallons of water a day from the tunnel below.

ABOVE **Permanent-way staff stand back to await the passage of a diesel railcar near Newbury on 10 July 1936. Quieter than steam locomotives, railcars posed more of a threat to track workers.**

the South Wales main line engineering work was normally carried out on winter Sundays between January and April each year. Just how busy the Severn Tunnel was is illustrated by the fact that, in 1937 alone, 23,808 trains passed through it; moreover, while passenger traffic was clearly important, the tunnel's role as an artery for South Wales coal traffic is clearly indicated by company statistics which record that 1,246,422 wagons were moved under the Severn that year — an average in excess of 52 per train. Work on the tunnel had therefore to be well planned and completed rapidly, in order to minimise disruption to passenger and freight timetables.

The engineers' occupation of the tunnel usually ran from 6am to 6pm and resulted in severe delays for passenger services; a large and comprehensive booklet was issued to staff each year, detailing all the alterations, diversions and cancellations of trains running to and from South Wales. Some long-distance passenger services were subject to substantial diversions; in 1922 the 4.55am Fishguard–Paddington express ran along the South Wales main line as far as Severn Tunnel Junction, from where it was diverted north along the Welsh side of the Severn to Gloucester; it then ran direct via Kemble before rejoining the main line at Swindon for the final leg of its journey to the capital, reaching Paddington at 11.30am. Passengers on stopping services from South Wales to Bristol fared even less well, their trains being diverted via Lydney and the old Severn Railway Bridge, crawling slowly across the Victorian structure and taking almost three hours to complete the journey.

In addition to the Sunday occupation the tunnel was often subject to speed restrictions in winter to allow maintenance work to continue, although a GWR memorandum issued in 1925 reveals that up and down lines were tackled separately in two distinct operations between the end of December and April. An article published in the *Great Western Railway Magazine* in 1932 provides some insight into the life of the permanent-way staff who worked in the tunnel on a day-to-day basis. Describing the work of the teams who were employed deep under the Severn, it records that there were recesses provided at 20yd intervals on alternate sides, providing for staff while trains passed, along with telephone boxes every half mile, allowing rapid communication with the signalboxes at each end of the tunnel. Most of the permanent-way men had worked for many years in the smoky darkness of the tunnel, the article concluded, noting that, no matter where they were within its 4½-mile length, they could tell when a train was entering by the 'instant effect' this had on the draught and its effect on their lamps.

The annual occupation was necessary not merely to inspect and repair the fabric of the tunnel itself but also to replace the rails that ran through it. The naturally damp conditions, coupled with the corrosive effect of locomotive smoke and fumes, meant that steel rail corroded far more quickly than in other, less-challenging locations on the network. As a result the track under the river was laid with special heavyweight rail designed for use in tunnels but still required replacing every two or three years, especially where heavy trains climbed out of the tunnel at the Bristol end. Even without the passage of trains, working in the tunnel during these annual occupations cannot have been a great experience for the permanent-way teams tasked with completing maintenance to tight deadlines each Sunday. Matters were improved a little in 1924 when a new ventilation fan was installed, replacing one brought into use 38 years earlier. The enormous new fan, powered by steam, measured 27ft in diameter and could pump 800,000cu ft of air into the tunnel per minute.

Installation the new fan of the new fan notwithstanding, in the years between the two world wars major maintenance work was required in the Severn Tunnel. Powerful pumps powered by massive Cornish beam engines installed at Sudbrook, Monmouthshire, ensured that it remained free of flooding even in the worst weather, but the erosion of the riverbed above the tunnel itself led to water seeping in from above. In 1925 the leakage was sufficient to require the company to keep carriage windows closed while trains passed through the tunnel, to avoid passengers' getting wet — or seriously alarmed by the amount of water present! Some idea of the quantities being pumped out of the tunnel can be gained from the fact that in 1935 that the maximum handled in a single day exceeded 36 million gallons, the minimum being just over 13 million.

Although the tunnel leak was initially sealed with a cap of clay this proved inadequate, and four years later a reinforced concrete top, known by staff as 'The Mushroom', was installed. Water continued to seep into the tunnel at the English end, due largely to the geological strata there, and in 1930 and 1931 the winter occupation was used to provide a more permanent solution to this problem. Staff from the Cementation Co used special equipment to pump a ring of special cement mixture through and behind the tunnel walls to create a waterproof barrier. This provided a better environment for the permanent-way staff

BELOW Besides warranting a mention in the company magazine the annual 'prize length' of permanent way was usually identified by a notice. This example, photographed in the 1950s, was at Llanbrynmair, in Mid Wales on the former Cambrian Lines.

ABOVE **The Wolverhampton Division weed-killing train, photographed on 20 April 1948.**

whose task it was to maintain the fabric of one of the most important structures on the railway and who, wrote W. G. Chapman, 'fearlessly followed their callings under the bed of the river for so many years in darkness, danger, and discomfort'.

Despite the weather the GWR maintained and ran ambitious excursion-train programmes, even in the depths of winter. This practice was reintroduced three years after the Great War, and in an editorial in the *Great Western Railway Magazine* for April 1921 the editor noted that day excursions had begun in February that year with trains to a number of sporting events, and that other day excursions to resorts and attractions 'had met with popular acclaim'.

Details of how far the running of winter excursions had developed between the wars is illustrated in a surviving booklet produced by the company in December 1937 outlining a series of Sunday trains proposed to run from Paddington and Ealing Broadway during January 1938. Listed over four pages numerous excursion destinations, from Aberdare to Yeovil; trains ran to Aberdare on the 2nd, 16th and 30th of the month, leaving Paddington at 9.35am. The South Wales train called at Newport and Cardiff and continued thence via Merthyr, arriving at Aberdare at 2.50 in the afternoon. The return service did not leave Aberdare until 12.35am, arriving back in London at 4.45 on Monday morning. The timetable also listed a train for Birkenhead Woodside which left Paddington at 9.30am, arriving at Birkenhead at 12.30pm; excursionists had almost 12 hours there, many doubtless taking the opportunity to travel on to Liverpool. The return train departed at 11.45pm and finally arrived back at Paddington at 5.25am; presumably the weary passengers had an hour or two to wash and have breakfast before beginning a day at work! The short winter days meant that there were no Cornish resorts listed in the excursion handbill; the most westerly point was Plymouth, which, even with a 9.30am departure, was not reached until 3pm, which in January would have meant that trippers would have had only a couple of hours of daylight there, and the 10.55pm return departure meant that many passengers, unless visiting friends or relations, would have spent much of their visit in a cinema or hostelry before making the long journey home, which concluded with a 4.35am arrival back in the capital.

The January handbill listed a good number of inland locations that required a rather shorter train journey, including many destinations in the Cotswolds, Devon, Somerset and Wiltshire. The last-mentioned also featured as a destination for a special 'Restaurant Car Half-Day Excursion' on 30 January 1938 which ran to Edington and Bratton on the West of England main line. A fulsome description of the ancient parish church in Edington was provided in the handbill, although what else excursionists could find to do in this relatively rural part of Wiltshire on a winter Sunday (apart from visiting the Westbury White Horse cut into the chalk of the downs nearby) is hard to imagine. Handbills were issued on a monthly basis and for most major stations across the network; specially priced tickets were offered for trips such as that to Edington, which cost 5s 9d for Third-class passengers; the Paddington–Birkenhead return trip cost 12s 6d. In addition, for those wishing to travel on ordinary scheduled trains on a Sunday, the railway offered Third-class return tickets for the cost of a single fare, First class being a little more expensive. Tickets were also valid for travel to destinations on the LMS and LNER, with a minimum ticket price of 2s 6d Third class and 3s 9d First.

The GWR's ever-resourceful publicity department also took the opportunity to advertise and run 'Long Distance Evening Excursions' in the winter. In January 1935 the company reported that it would be offering 'exceptionally cheap' evening travel facilities over longer distances than before, having provided bargain fares for local services for many years. The Bristol–Paddington train left Temple Meads station at 5pm, reaching the capital two hours later; the return journey left Paddington at 11pm, giving excursionists time to see the sights, have a meal or take in a show for just 5s. Similar long-distance evening trains were run from Bristol to Birmingham, Hereford to Birmingham and Oswestry to Liverpool.

The GWR workforce took advantage of dark winter evenings to hold all manner of dinners, especially before and after the Christmas and New Year break; during the winter period the *Great Western Railway Magazine* was always full of long and detailed articles giving details of gatherings large and small. Dinners were held by individual stations, divisions and departments, and the March 1928 edition reported on dinners held at Plymouth, Swansea, Manchester, Birkenhead, Lostwithiel, Totnes and Tyseley, for a variety of different organisations. The largest, with more than 100 staff and guests attending, was held by the clerical staff of the Goods Department at Birkenhead and Liverpool, while the smallest, for just 40, was for station staff at Totnes, at which event, the magazine noted, a 'happy social spirit' prevailed under the chairmanship of stationmaster Mr W. Gale.

Events held in London for the various departments of the company based in and around Paddington were normally rather larger and grander affairs than those held by staff elsewhere on the railway; it was recorded that 'all previous records were broken' at the annual dinner and concert of the Superintendent of the Line held on 28 January 1938, when 270 people gathered at the Chiltern Hall, in Baker Street. Dinners such as these were an opportunity for staff past and present to meet and reminisce, and on this occasion the Superintendent of the Line, Mr F. R. Potter, was careful to toast his predecessor, Mr R. H. Nicholls, and wish him 'continued good health and happy retirement'. The Chiltern Hall was the venue for another dinner a week or so later, this time for the Chief Goods Manager's Office, an event attracting more than 280 diners. There were no speeches, reported the *Great Western Railway Magazine*; instead there was 'an excellent

BELOW Despite the use of some equipment to assist them, the task of lifting a length of rail into place was back-breaking work and one which required at least eight men to complete, as this image shows.

LEFT **The cover of a GWR booklet aimed at improving safety for permanent-way staff, first published in 1936 and re-issued after World War 2.**

programme of entertainment' including renditions by the GWR Goods Department 'Glee Singers'. The guest list for the dinner was, however, a veritable 'Who's Who' of the company, including the Chief Accountant, Chief Civil Engineer, Superintendent of the Line, Assistant General Manager, Publicity Officer and the stationmaster at Paddington as well as others from outside the GWR, such as the editor of the *Railway Gazette*.

For GWR management an important early winter landmark was the completion of accounts and other information for the annual report that was discussed and debated at the Annual General Meeting, usually held in February. The Company Chairman gave a commentary to both the report and the annual accounts, and this provided an opportunity for shareholders to question management about the running of the company. The number of people holding shares in the Great Western was considerable; in 1923 it was noted that there were nearly 120,000 stockholders, a figure that had increased from 95,000 following the Grouping. Of this total around half had investments of less than £500 in the company. As a result attendance at the annual meeting, although healthy, normally numbered around 200; not surprisingly, more shareholders were present at meetings held at times of financial difficulty for the railway, particularly in the years after the Great War and leading up to the Grouping and for some years thereafter. A somewhat irreverent article published in the *Great Western Railway Magazine* in 1932 provides an interesting insight into the AGM; Sir Robert Perks, a railway lawyer and someone whose family had 'a considerable stake' in the railway's fortunes, provided what the magazine called a 'shareholder's viewpoint'. Perks told readers that when he had attended a meeting some years earlier it was 'held in a small hall which was packed to suffocation', adding that the air was 'intolerable' and further noting that the Chairman's address, 'which was read from end to end', was 'terribly dull, possibly as a result of the atmosphere, and very long'. The magazine usually reproduced the remarks made by the Chairman at the AGM, so it would have been interesting to know his reaction to the article.

On occasions the *Great Western Railway Magazine* included some of the questions asked by shareholders. Perks noted that, at the meeting he attended, 'a few desultory questions, mainly of local interest, were put by exhausted shareholders' before the proceedings closed, but it appears that in later years, while there were always some questions posed by investors with particular local issues to air, most were of a broader nature. In 1931 and 1932 the GWR reproduced a selection of questions and the responses from the Company Chairman. Not surprisingly, many shareholders were keen for the railway to reduce its costs, as ultimately this might improve the level of dividend paid; perhaps with this in mind, in 1931 one Mr Short thought that 'a board of 25 Directors of any company, let alone the GWR, was unworkable'. Responding, the Chairman said that the higher number of directors was due partly to the 1923 Grouping process, but, from his experience of 20 years, 'work would not be so efficiently done if we reduced the number of directors'. Another common theme was staff costs, and the following year Mr W. H. Robson raised the issue of railway wages, which, he felt, were 'far too high' and out of proportion with other trades; he also thought that railwaymen took their 'privileges' for granted. The Chairman, noting these concerns, told Robson that wage levels were set nationally and that the company had only a limited influence on pay rates. With less concern for profitability, in 1932 the Rev C. Lefroy told the meeting that 'he was afraid that the Directors did not appreciate the psychological value of cheapness', suggesting that ordinary passenger fares be substantially reduced and, if this were to be done, it should be 'well advertised'. The Chairman gently reminded the clergyman that, however worthy this move might

ABOVE **One of a series used to warn staff of the dangers of working on the line; this posed photograph shows 'Hall' 4-6-0 No 5925 *Eastcote Hall* seemingly about to run over an unwitting ganger.**

have been, it would have had a serious effect on the finances of the company, as 40% of its income was generated from passenger fares. The same meeting generated a variety of other questions and comments, including one about the transport of pork and flowers from Cornwall and the Isles of Scilly and a point raised by Mr F. G. Cannon that the company was potentially losing money through its failure to print telephone numbers on traffic advices, visiting cards and other official documents.

Perks noted that a 'new custom had come into vogue' — that of printing the Chairman's speech in *The Times* and other newspapers. The justification for this costly expenditure, he continued, was that it saved the GWR 'the expenses of printing the proceedings in a pamphlet and posting to each shareholder'. This may well have been the case, but while some individuals and groups of shareholders might well have had occasional misgivings

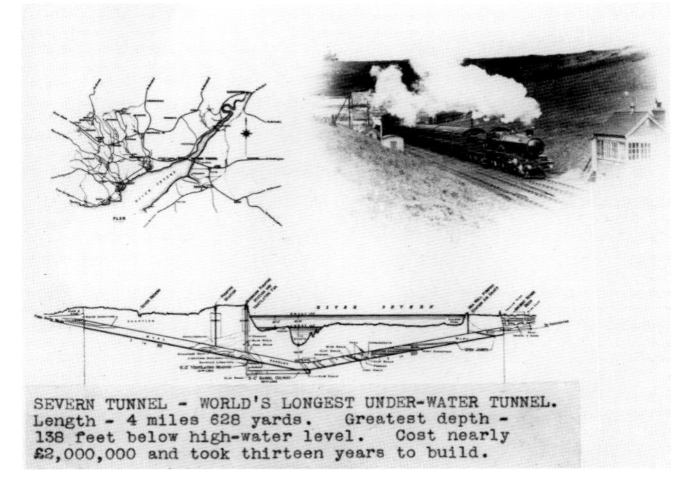

ABOVE **A publicity photograph of the Severn Tunnel, along with a cross-sectional diagram and a map showing its location, released by the GWR in the 1930s.**

LEFT **Permanent-way staff were required to check track whatever the weather. This ganger is carrying both a large hammer, for ensuring track keys are in place, and a large spanner, for tightening bolts.**

TOP RIGHT **Comptometer operators in the Machine Service Office of the Chief Mechanical Engineer's Department at Swindon in the late 1930s. Information recorded here was used to provide statistics for GWR management at Swindon and Paddington.** *Alan Wakefield collection*

BOTTOM RIGHT **Daffodils being prepared at a Cornish nursery in the 1920s.**

over the way in which the railway was run and the level of income and expenditure generated during the interwar period, they were nevertheless still able to enjoy dividends that were rather better than those paid by the other 'Big Four' companies.

Perks complained that, as a shareholder, he was 'perplexed and concerned', noting that 'In the distribution of earnings of railway enterprises the shareholders get nothing until everybody else had been paid' and reminding the readers of the magazine that without shareholder cash the railway could not continue to generate income. In the 20 years between 1919 and 1939, however, the dividend did not drop below 3%, not even in the year of the General Strike. As a result most shareholders were content to allow the GWR's board of directors to act on their behalf in appointing the company's most senior officers and approving the most important matters relating to its business. The company magazine reported that the first meeting after the Grouping in 1923 was attended by 'an unusually large number of shareholders', who must have been somewhat relieved to hear how, despite the fact that the railway and its associated costs had grown considerably, prospects for its future were highly satisfactory, the Chairman telling them that 'there was every reason to be hopeful as regards the future'.

Staff and travellers standing on a draughty platform at Paddington late on a cold winter's night might well have caught a glimpse of some of the thousands of boxes of Cornish flowers being unloaded at the station ready to be transported to the market at Covent Garden. The mild climate in Cornwall and the Isles of Scilly, which the GWR was so keen to promote as the reason for a winter holiday, also provided the conditions necessary for a large and important flower-growing industry, which had developed following the arrival of the railway in West Cornwall in 1859. With railway connections, flowers and vegetables grown in the Isles of Scilly and the Royal Duchy could be conveyed quickly and profitably to London and other markets on the British mainland.

'When spring comes to the rest of England the Cornish flower season is almost over,' noted a 1938 *Great Western Railway Magazine* article on the flower trade; because of the mild climate in coastal areas flowers could be grown out of doors and were ready for harvest earlier, realising higher prices than what the GWR called 'up-country' crops. The main flowers grown were daffodils, irises, tulips and anemones (although the last were a relatively recent innovation), and by 1938 more than 13 million bunches were being grown annually. Each season more than a thousand tons of flowers were brought from the Isles of Scilly to Penzance by boat, blooms being available there two or three weeks earlier than Cornwall; the mild conditions on the islands meant that narcissi and anemones could be picked in December, although most traffic was generated after New Year. This was a welcome boost to winter freight; the quantity of flowers sent by the GWR was reported as being between three and four thousand tons annually, a significant amount. The harvest could, however, be affected by parasitic disease and rot in plants and bulbs, and in 1938, in a move that reflected the importance of the trade to the company, the railway provided a grant to support research for growers. Despite competition from other parts of the country, notably Lincolnshire, the 'fresh and sturdy open-air flowers of Cornwall' were more than holding their own, it was reported, and the appearance every year of this bright and attractive traffic must have provided GWR staff with the thought and hope that spring was on its way and that the dark, cold and difficult winter months were almost over.

GREAT WESTERN GOODS

In the foreword to its 1936 publication *The GWR Guide to Economical Transport* the company argued that the purpose of the book was to give details of 'the manifold services and facilities placed by the Great Western Railway at the disposal of its customers'. It further suggested that the railway had made 'cheapness, rapidity and convenience its specialised study' and that it was always prepared to adapt its services to meet the needs of any industry. The aim was, it concluded, to provide 'the right type of service at the right price', adding that the company could always 'arrange a rapid, safe, and cheap method of conveyance for all classes of freight traffic'. Laudable though this statement was, it was nevertheless a source of considerable frustration to the management of the GWR (and indeed the other 'Big Four' companies) that, unlike the many road haulage firms that had sprung up following the Great War, railways were classed as 'common carriers'. This role, which was embedded into the Parliamentary legislation that enabled them to operate, meant that they had to carry any form of commodity or goods brought to a station or goods depot for transport, whatever the

BELOW This view of the goods depot at Bristol in the 1920s illustrates just how varied and busy was the GWR's freight business. Horse-drawn delivery vehicles are still much in evidence, although a number of motor lorries can be seen in the background.

ABOVE A train of 20-ton coal wagons (as introduced by the company between the wars) stand ready at one of the GWR's South Wales docks; older, wooden coal wagons can be seen on the far left of the picture.

type, size or weight. Exactly what could be carried was contained in the 'General Classification of Merchandise', which, the company noted, was a list or book containing the names, in alphabetical order, of thousands of articles regularly forwarded by rail. These items were grouped into various categories for the purpose of determining how much it would cost to transport them.

During the 1920s and 1930s goods traffic could be broadly (though not exclusively) divided into two types, the first being general merchandise that included smaller consignments of freight that either were large enough to fill an entire wagon or constituted 'sundry' traffic that was carried as a mixed load; the second was bulk traffic, whereby large tonnages of freight were moved by the railway, often in faster, vacuum-braked trains. As road competition increased, the GWR found it more difficult to compete with the convenience offered by motor lorries, especially for general merchandise. The conveyance of bulk traffic provided more opportunities for the GWR, which could compete better against road transport, as fast trunk roads and motorways had yet to be developed. The company had therefore to provide special rolling stock and devise working practices necessary to deal with various types of traffic. Space does not permit a comprehensive survey of all the loads handled, but this chapter will describe a selection of both the staple and the more unusual traffic, as well as some of the wagons provided to transport these loads and some of the ways in which the goods were handled subsequently; special seasonal loads are described elsewhere in the book.

Most of the wagons mentioned are described using the code names assigned by the company in its Telegraphic Code book. This included well over 900 code words, a significant number of which provided concise and accurate descriptions of its rolling stock; the GWR assigned code names to each wagon type, and these were then used in telegraph messages sent between stations and depots. The name, which usually appeared on the side of the vehicle, was sometimes straightforward, as in the case of 'Grano', describing a wagon used to transport grain, but in most cases random and rather exotic names were applied. The humble covered merchandise wagon, for example, was codenamed 'Mink', while the wagons used for moving heavy equipment were coded 'Crocodile'.

Between the two world wars one of the most important loads carried by the railway was coal. Following the Grouping the GWR, which already carried thousands of tons of coal from South Wales, found itself owning and managing companies like the Taff Vale, Rhymney and Cardiff railways, which hitherto had been profitable operations whose *raison d'être* was coal. In its own publication *Commerce and the Great Western Railway*, published in 1924, the company recorded that, in addition to the South Wales Coalfield, it served collieries in 'North Wales, the Forest of Dean,

ABOVE **Loaded and empty china-clay wagons are in evidence in this 1930s view of the GWR facility at Fowey, Cornwall.**

South Staffordshire and Somersetshire'. Coal production had doubled in the two decades before the Great War, and it was hoped that following the end of the conflict the coal trade would provide a steady and growing source of income for the company. GWR publicity boasted that the 'world-famous' mineral deposits of South Wales covered more than 1,000 square miles and included bituminous coal suitable for use in blast furnaces and foundries, as well as steam coal and anthracite — a variety that was 'indispensable' to markets in Canada and the United States. The expected postwar boom in the coal business did not materialise, however, and the combined effects of the miners' strike and General Strike of 1926, followed by the Great Depression, led to a sharp drop in coal production from which the industry did not fully recover before the outbreak of World War 2 in 1939. The Great Western strove to ameliorate the loss of income that was a consequence of the slump in the coal trade, offering attractive discounts to colliery owners and iron and steel manufacturers and also investing large sums in new equipment at ports to expedite the loading of coal for export, but efforts to persuade colliery owners to invest in larger and more efficient 20-ton wagons were less successful than had been hoped.

Many of the heavy loads carried by the GWR were linked to the industries located on its network in North and South Wales, Staffordshire, Shropshire, Wolverhampton and Birmingham. The iron and steel trade was second only to coal in South Wales, and from Newport in the east to Llanelly in the west there were many businesses that relied on the supply of raw materials by the railway. In the 1920s more than 1,500,000 tons of iron ore and steel bar was imported annually through GWR docks and then loaded into wagons for delivery to foundries, steelworks and factories. A 1939 guide to GWR port facilities noted that 'the iron and steel products of South Wales are of the most varied description and include practically every commodity in the trade'. These products included steel rail, point work and sleepers, galvanised-iron sheets, tubes, pipes, boilers and all manner of other items; many of the largest and heaviest items products were loaded on to large GWR bogie wagons with the telegraphic code 'Crocodile'. There were various designs of this wagon type, including the 'Crocodile L' variation, which was the largest to run

ABOVE The mechanised tipping equipment provided at Fowey made loading ships with china clay a relatively straightforward operation, but it was a dusty process, as will be apparent from the state of the workmen's clothing in this photograph.

on the network and often used for outsize loads. The railway made much of its ability to handle these 'exceptional loads', its 1936 *Guide to Economical Transport* noting pointedly that railways, 'unlike many of the highways of this country', had been specially constructed to withstand the conveyance of 'tremendous weights at high speeds', also describing the special arrangements that might be required to move a heavy or awkward load, including the occupation of two running lines simultaneously and alterations to track or lineside structures to permit the passage of a special train. The *Great Western Railway Magazine* of the period often reported on the movement of unusual and exceptional loads such as electrical transformers, large castings, bridge girders, boilers, guns and large industrial machinery.

Other wagons were used for particular traffic; for the movement of steel tubes long-wheelbase 22-ton open wagons were provided, these being fitted on each side with double doors that could be dropped down to facilitate the unloading of pipes or tubes. Other products of South Wales steel mills included steel wire and steel strip coil; the former tended to be loaded into standard four-plank open wagons, whilst the latter was transported after World War 2 in large (42-ton) steel bogie wagons. In addition to traffic generated in South Wales the industrial powerhouse of the West Midlands was a source of huge revenue to the GWR, in terms of the transportation of raw materials from South Wales ports and the movement of manufactured products in the opposite direction.

Perhaps the most distinctive mineral traffic carried by the GWR was china clay; described as the 'white gold of Cornwall', the white clay, more correctly known as Kaolin, had been exploited commercially in the Duchy for more than 200 years and by the 1930s was (and indeed continues to be) used for the manufacture of porcelain, pottery and paper. Although extraction began in the 18th century it was not until the 1850s that the industry developed significantly. Railways were used to transport china clay to the coast for export from the 1840s, and the creation of the Cornwall Minerals Railway in 1873 led to the construction of a new line from Par to Fowey, where a deep-water port was established.

ABOVE **Open wagons being moved using a capstan rather than horse or locomotive power at the GWR goods depot at Hockley, Birmingham.**

Initially there were three wooden jetties provided for the loading of china clay, but further expansion in 1890 saw the addition of a further jetty and facilities for the loading of china clay in casks.

A network of branch lines in the area of china-clay production around St Austell fed the Cornish port of Fowey with loaded trains on a daily basis; by the outbreak of World War 1 this had become the main china-clay-exporting port in the world, and more than half of the total output of the industry in Cornwall passed through it. To cope with this high level of business the GWR embarked upon an ambitious scheme to update the facilities at the port, a project that was interrupted by hostilities and not completed until 1923. The china-clay industry was badly affected by the war, and the completion of modernisation work at Fowey fortuitously coincided with an upturn in business. When complete the refurbished facility was provided with three main jetties with a total frontage of more than 2,400ft, each jetty equipped with electric conveyor belts enabling china clay to be shifted quickly from railway wagon to the hold of a ship; the old wooden jetties remained in use to handle bagged clay. New cranes were also provided, along with electric capstans used to shunt wagons on the quay, replacing the horses that had done this job previously. Company records reveal that in 1914 the china clay handled at Fowey amounted to 595,565 tons; by 1923 this total had grown to 659,237 tons, and the Great Western's guide to its dock facilities for 1939 noted that the previous year's exports of china clay had exceeded 800,000 tons, while boasting that it was designed to deal with a million tons per annum if required.

Clay was brought to Fowey in various forms — highly refined powder clay, ball clay (in large lumps) and china stone. In the case of the powder clay special wagons with end doors were provided, and on arrival on the dockside these were shunted onto tipper platforms that could be tilted, allowing the clay to be unloaded from the wagon onto the conveyor belt below. The wagons were also fitted with zinc sheets covering the floor planks, as the transport of the clay caused serious wet rot; the smooth zinc surface also made unloading of the clay easier at the port. In the 1920s '42xx' 2-8-0 tank engines were introduced to St Blazey shed, replacing smaller six-coupled tanks; built primarily for hauling coal trains in South Wales, these locomotives were more than capable of hauling 22 10-ton china-clay wagons over the steeper sections of the branch lines in the St Austell area. Reporting on the GWR operation at Fowey in 1937, the company magazine described china clay as 'prosaic stuff' but 'ubiquitous in the life of the community', concluding that passengers journeying through the scenic delights of Cornwall were largely unaware of the scale of the operation at the port or of the impact on daily life of its principal export.

Another basic commodity carried by the Great Western was wood, in all its forms, from large trees to sawn and baulk timbers. Ports in South Wales, notably Cardiff, were centres for the import and distribution of thousands of tons of wood and what was then called 'mining timber'. The GWR ran regular trains from the docks to coal mines in the Valleys and the Midlands, delivering pit props and wood. In 1929 the company estimated that more than half a million tons of wood for this purpose was imported into Cardiff alone, pit wood being imported from Scandinavia (notably Finland) and Russia in the summer months and from France, Spain and Portugal all year round. Timber of all kinds arrived from such as France, Norway, Sweden, Finland, the Baltic states and Canada and made a significant contribution to the company's revenue. In 1927 more than 279,000 tons of timber and deals was handled by all the docks in South Wales, timber for pit use adding a further 1,100,000 tons to this overall total. By 1937 the effects of the Depression on the coal trade meant that the quantity of general timber handled by the company had increased to over 350,000 tons while the amount of pit wood imported had dropped to around 750,000 tons. If of an equal height, the thousands of pit props moved from port to pit were normally stacked vertically in standard GWR open wagons; loads such as sawn timber and floorboards needed rather more care to ensure that the wood was safely loaded and secured, and a number of pages in the *General Appendix to the Rule Book* issued to staff were dedicated to this task. The variety of what the railway termed 'other timber' was considerable; a 1939 guide to dock facilities on the GWR gave an extensive list of the woods unloaded and then moved by the railway. Included in this list were hewn oak logs, ash, hickory, yellow pine and greenheart from

BELOW Unloading pit wood from a Breton schooner at Swansea Docks in March 1924.

ABOVE LEFT **Large logs loaded on a GWR wagon at Plymouth on 16 June 1903.**

ABOVE RIGHT **The railway also handled large quantities of sawn and machined timber. This wagonload was photographed at Newport on 30 June 1903. These views were taken to show how the loads had moved in transit.**

RIGHT **Grain being loaded into one of a fleet of 12 wagons built for a service between Birkenhead and Wrexham, inaugurated in 1927.**

Quebec and ebony, walnut, mahogany, redwood and teak from South East Asia and South America, as well as prepared boards, railway sleepers of all kinds, laths, boards and staves.

The company provided various special 'Macaw' bogie wagons to carry larger and longer logs and could handle loads up to 90ft long, although these were the exception rather than the rule and had to be carefully routed to avoid tight curves. Not all the wood handled by the company came from exotic locations; an article published in the *Great Western Railway Magazine* in 1931 gave details of the railway's operations in Central Wales, where forestry was one of the main industries. Up to 30,000 tons of wood were moved by rail from the area annually, the 'round' timber including oak, elm, ash, beech, sycamore, larch and spruce. The often remote nature of the area meant that much effort was required on the part of forestry workers to fell trees and prepare them for transit and also to haul them considerable distances to stations where they could be loaded. In a number of cases forests were almost completely inaccessible by road, and the article gave details of the great efforts made by the GWR to enable timber to be loaded directly on the running line. In view of the day-to-day pressures of running a regular passenger service this operation could not take place on a weekday, so loading usually took place on Sundays. The company went to great lengths to expedite such activity, a number of departments being involved; in addition to involvement of Goods staff, in most cases the Engineering Department was called upon to remove fencing from the lineside, and the Chief Mechanical Engineer's Department was required to supply hand or steam cranes to lift timber onto waiting wagons, while the Signal Department might also be called upon to remove telegraph wires if these were likely to impede loading. Careful preparation ensured that loading could be completed as quickly as possible, and the article reported the successful loading and transportation, on behalf of a Welshpool timber merchant, of a train of almost 100 tons of oak and larch, some of the trees weighing between 6 and 7 tons each, to which were added 34 tons of pit props loaded into five wagons by staff from the timber company. Although the GWR was, of course, paid to undertake such work the report nevertheless underlines the railway's commitment to generating business and meeting its customer's requirements.

The three major ports for the importation of barley, flour, maize, wheat and other grain traffic were Barry, Cardiff and

G
W
42243
BIRKENHEA & WREXHAM
RETURN TO
G.W.R

Swansea, and in the 1930s imports of these crops amounted to more than 500,000 tons a year. Although large flour mills were built close to all three ports grain was despatched from a number of other docks; the company had facilities at Birkenhead for unloading imported grain and transporting it to a flour mill at Wrexham, as well as a smaller operation at Millbay, Plymouth, where in 1939 around 125,000 tons of grain was 'expeditiously discharged', the company reported. In 1927 the GWR built a dozen new wooden grain wagons for the Birkenhead–Wrexham service. These hopper wagons could be loaded through an aperture in the roof and then discharged their load of grain through a hopper underneath the wagon. In 1935/6, however, they were replaced in bulk-grain traffic by an all-steel 20-ton design that featured two roof apertures, to speed loading.

While the GWR needed to take great care in moving fragile and perishable goods such as fruit and vegetables, even greater care was required in the movement of livestock. In addition to the racehorse traffic described in Part 4 the company moved large numbers of cattle around the system. The business could be divided broadly into two parts, the first being the import of cattle from abroad into its docks, their reception and then despatch to other parts of the country, the second the handling of the domestic cattle trade, moving animals from farms to markets and slaughterhouses from its own stations. Large consignments of cattle from Canada and South Africa were dealt with at Cardiff, where the facilities were licensed by the Government and special purpose-built berthing and pens provided, with water and feed. An auction ring was also installed, ensuring that cattle could be processed quickly after arrival and loaded onto rail vehicles as soon as possible. A *Great Western Railway Magazine* article written in 1932 reported that cattle importation through Cardiff had in recent years been a rather intermittent business, this being due largely to shortages of livestock in the United States which had seen Canada's exports diverted there. However, imports to Cardiff resumed in June 1932 and continued to be a useful source of income to the company.

The company's harbour at Fishguard was also an important part of a significant cattle trade between Ireland and Great Britain. It was noted in 1922 that the Irish cattle trade had 'progressed in a truly remarkable way' and that the provision of new purpose-built facilities at Fishguard (completed in 1906) and also the use of GWR steamships that could handle up to 500 head of cattle on each crossing had made no small contribution to the growth of the trade. The sea crossing was not always the smoothest, especially in the winter months, and as a result ample accommodation was provided at the port, allowing cattle a 10-hour quarantine and

BELOW It seems likely that GWR station staff would not have looked forward to unloading this bull, who looks less than happy about his incarceration in one of the company's cattle wagons.

inspection period before being loaded onto trains for markets as far away as Bristol and Norwich. Inspection by Ministry of Agriculture vets was vitally important, as the Irish cattle trade was hit by a number of foot-and-mouth outbreaks during the interwar period. Business was also affected by the political instability that resulted from the creation of the Irish Free State.

Some idea of the size of the GWR's cattle business can be gained from the fact that between 1888 and 1904 the company had built some 1,250 8-ton 'Mex' cattle wagons. Between 1929 and 1933 a further 240 cattle wagons of a similar design were built at Swindon, still more being produced in the early days of nationalisation. The 18ft-long vehicle had a moveable partition inside that could change the interior layout; this partition was required to enable mixed consignments of livestock to be handled. Whilst this was clearly a more cost-effective option for the company, great care had to be taken in the way such loads were arranged. GWR regulations provided some guidance for staff, noting that 'small animals must not be loaded with large ones' and that a cow with its unweaned calf could travel together, 'provided they are separated from other animals'. Staff were also advised that 'owing to their fighting propensities, pigs must not be loaded with sheep or calves'.

ABOVE A horse (just visible at the bottom of the photograph) awaits loading at Paddington on 8 June 1930. Two cattle wagons are stabled in the sidings beyond, along with a variety of other GWR freight wagons, including a 'Toad' brake van from Weymouth.

For special pedigree cattle the company built a larger wagon, codenamed 'Beetle', which was similar to a horsebox. This wagon, which was vacuum-fitted to enable it to be run as part of a passenger train, had a passenger compartment in the middle where a farm-hand or owner could keep an eye on the six animals the van could hold. All bulls and 'horned livestock' carried in the same vehicle as a bull were to be securely tied by the head or neck, according to company regulations. The movement of cattle and other livestock was part of the day-to-day life at country stations, and most had cattle pens and loading facilities that were used on a regular basis, although the growth of road competition began to reduce the amount of traffic handled in the 1920s and 1930s. The Great Western issued detailed instructions to its staff on the handling of live animals, noting that 'care and patience must be shown, not only in loading and unloading' but also in the treatment of them 'during transit, in and about the yards, pens and stations'. This was, the regulations continued, 'to avoid fright

ABOVE **In addition to road vehicles used for the collection and delivery of goods and parcels the GWR owned numerous lorries that could be used as part of its Country Lorry service to transport farm livestock to and from stations.**

or injury and consequent suffering on the part of the animals'. The company needed to ensure that it adhered to the various Government regulations surrounding the care and movement of livestock, but no doubt it also wanted to minimise any claims from farmers or stock-owners for compensation for ill-treatment of animals. While there was no specific regulation requiring railways to feed animals during a journey, to avoid undue suffering all the 'Big Four' companies adopted guidelines which saw that horses and donkeys were fed at least every 24 hours, cattle and pigs every 27 hours, and sheep and lambs every 36 hours. GWR regulations also noted that 'every station at which animals are habitually loaded, unloaded, or detained during transit' should 'make provision of water for the animals carried'.

Care was also required to prevent disease, especially foot-and-mouth, and the company's instructions to staff at stations were extremely detailed and clear. After use cattle wagons, road vehicles and station pens were to be thoroughly cleaned and 'disinfected by being thoroughly coated or washed with an approved disinfectant'. Wagons and pens had traditionally been treated with lime wash, but concerns over its effectiveness as a disinfecting agent following a number of serious outbreaks of disease and issues surrounding animal welfare led to its prohibition in 1927 and replacement with phenol-based disinfectant. The GWR was required to take great care when transporting livestock generally; 'movement orders' were issued by local authorities in order to prevent the spread of swine fever and sheep scab, and stationmasters and goods-yard staff were required to make careful checks of licences and paperwork supplied by farmers before loading animals for transport to locations elsewhere on the network.

With a network that included lines serving numerous ports and harbours in the South West of England and South Wales, the GWR generated a good deal of income from fish traffic. In Cornwall the railways had long played an important role in the development of the fishing industry, giving it rapid access to growing markets in London and the Midlands. As the industry grew in the Victorian era smaller Cornish ports became less influential, and following the end of World War 1 Newlyn, with its modern facilities and connection to the GWR, had become the most important fishing port in the West Country; in 1919 it was handling 31% of the entire catch for the region, a figure that 20 years later had grown to 51%.

Great Western stations and depots in West Wales also handled significant amounts of fish traffic. Adrian Vaughan records that the company ran four fish trains daily from Fishguard Harbour, all carrying fish brought by ship from Ireland. Two trains ran to the North of England via the LMS line to Crewe, the others via Swansea to various destinations on the GWR network. Regular services also ran from another Pembrokeshire port, Milford Haven; although when the regular trawler fleet based there moved to the East Coast of England in 1931 the boats that replaced them continued to work out of the port, and by the mid-1930s more than 40,000 tons of fish were being landed at Milford every year. Although the principal South Wales docks of Swansea and Cardiff were better known for the export of coal and the import of other general merchandise both were significant contributors to the fish trade. In 1939 the company reported that more than 10,000 tons of fish were landed at Swansea by Consolidated Fisheries Ltd, whose company's trawlers were berthed at the South Dock. Besides a fish market an ice factory was provided to service the trade, and a similar facility was provided at Cardiff, where the docks dealt with the importation of 6,000 tons of fish every year. The ice was used to pack fish into wooden boxes, which once sold were weighed, labelled and loaded by GWR staff into wagons for transport. Handling the wet and slimy boxes must have been one of the most difficult and unpleasant jobs on the railway, especially as speed was of the essence; fish trains were vacuum-braked and run as fast as possible to ensure that the highly perishable load reached its destination in good time.

Despite some difficulties in the years immediately following World War 1, when both had struggled for survival, by the late 1920s the fortunes of the Austin and Morris car companies had improved significantly. Production at factories such as the Morris Motors facility at Cowley in Oxford and the Austin plant at Longbridge in Birmingham began to increase, cars being built for both the domestic and export markets. By 1939 Morris had built its 1,000,000th car, and despite the fact that the revolution in car ownership was beginning to erode its own passenger business the Great Western had little choice but to try to secure as much business as possible from car companies wishing to transport

ABOVE Pictured on 19 October 1921, '43xx' Mogul No 5347 stands at the head of an express fish train comprising six 'Bloater' wagons, a bogie open fish wagon and an eight-wheel brake van.

BELOW A 'Bocar' bogie wagon used to transport Morris car bodies, photographed on 22 January 1936.

ABOVE The scene at Pilning High Level station in July 1958, with a car loaded for transit through the Severn Tunnel. *H. C. Casserley collection*

RIGHT Built on the site of Garsington Bridge Halt, the new Morris Cowley station was opened on 24 September 1928. Close by were sidings serving the growing motor factory; there was however, still some work to do when this photograph was taken. *British Motor Industry Heritage Trust*

finished vehicles, especially for export. Facilities at Cowley were expanded significantly in July 1928, when the two sidings provided two years earlier for the Pressed Steel body plant were augmented by a further five lines. A new station, named Morris Cowley, was opened later the same year, enabling the GWR to run workmen's trains for Morris company staff.

Such was the growth in motor-car traffic that in 1930 the *Great Western Railway Magazine* reported that 'for some time past there has been an increasing call for vehicles for conveyance of motor cars, arising in no small part from the successful efforts to secure this business to rail'. It was noted that existing stock for transporting cars had been in great demand and that only through 'considerable ingenuity' had it been possible to meet the requirements of car companies. The solution to these difficulties — and a possible increase in demand — was, the article continued, the construction of 100 new covered motor-car wagons. Codenamed 'Asmo', these large (32ft 8in) wagons were capable of carrying two motor cars and were fitted with end doors and gas lighting; cross-beams and large leather restraining straps were also provided, to prevent any movement of the cars while in transit. The wagons were also vacuum-braked, enabling them to be used on express services.

In 1933 Swindon began to build shorter-wheelbase wagons especially for the transportation of motor vehicles from manufacturers to distributors or ports. Closely resembling the thousands of 12-ton standard ventilated wagons used by the company, the 'Mogo' variation differed in having, like the 'Asmo', end doors and a drop flap, enabling cars to be easily loaded. In three years 350 wagons of this type were constructed, to be followed by a further batch built in 1946/7. Morris and other motor companies also developed the idea of CKD (completely knocked-down) cars, which were in essence kits of parts for export. To carry the car bodies, which were exported all over the British Empire, the GWR provided 111 bogie wagons that were capable of carrying eight car bodies loaded sideways; these 'Bocar' wagons were not new, however, instead consisting of old clerestory-carriage underframes topped with a relatively lightweight steel framework fitted with tarpaulin sides. Most Morris cars were sent to the Great Western's dock at Brentford, from where they were moved by barge to London docks for export, yielding the railway an income of £3,500 per year; vehicles were also moved to South Wales ports and to Scotland. The GWR also worked with the LMS to transport Austin cars from the Longbridge plant to London and Glasgow.

In an echo of a service provided in the broad-gauge era, when horse-drawn carriages had been transported on wagons attached to passenger trains, the GWR also offered car owners the opportunity to have their vehicles transported long distances by passenger train. In 1927, 'in view of the tremendous growth of motor-touring', the company advertised the reduction of its mileage rates for this traffic by one third, the reduction being 'for the benefit of people on holiday who wish to take their cars with them, but prefer not to drive long distances', according to a *Great Western Railway Magazine* correspondent. A broadly similar service was provided for motorists wishing to avoid a long and tortuous drive up the east side of the Severn Estuary from Bristol to Gloucester and back down the west side of the river into South Wales; instead they could travel to Pilning, or Severn Tunnel Junction on the Welsh side and make use of flat wagons stabled there that could be coupled onto the next convenient stopping passenger service for a rather quicker trip through the Severn Tunnel.

One load not usually carried through the Severn Tunnel was explosives. As a common carrier the GWR was obliged to transport even the most dangerous of loads, and not surprisingly its rule book provided considerable guidance to staff. In general, gunpowder and other explosives were moved around the network in four-wheeled iron 'Mink' wagons that were lined with wood to reduce the risk of any sparks' causing an explosion during loading and unloading. For the same reason each of these vans was also provided with a pair of 'Gunpowder Boots' which had no nails in their soles. These 'nail-less' boots were issued by the General Stores at Swindon Works 'to protect staff engaged in loading and unloading explosives', the company magazine reported; rather than being issued individual members of staff they were instead to 'travel with the gunpowder van wherever it goes, on hooks purposely provided'. The *General Appendix to the Rule Book* noted that, for added security, the doors of vans carrying explosives were fitted with locks, the keys being retained at stations that handled this dangerous load on a regular basis. There were also copious instructions on how to deal with derailments and fires on trains containing explosives or other hazardous loads; wagons containing explosives or flammable substances were to be placed as far as practicable from the locomotive, and at all times the instruction 'Shunt with Care' was to be adhered to!

ABOVE A 1938 photograph showing the interior of a GWR 'Mink' gunpowder wagon, complete with numerous notices warning staff of the hazardous load being carried.

There were, of course, numerous consignments that did not fit into any of the specific categories of goods traffic already described, such loads being usually carried in the variety of open wagons and wooden 'Mink' vans that were normally marshalled in mixed goods trains. The correct loading of these wagons was vitally important to prevent damage to goods and subsequent insurance claims from customers, and the *General Appendix* reminded goods foremen, loaders, shunters and guards that they should 'take the utmost care to see that the contents of all wagons are evenly distributed, safely and properly loaded and secured where necessary'. That damage sustained by rough handling in both loading and unloading continued to be a major problem is evinced by the stream of warnings issued by the company to its staff in its weekly general instructions. These illustrate not only its concern over losses but also the huge variety of goods transported; in 1927 staff were told that 'strong complaints have been received regarding damage to consignments of ladies hats packed in cardboard boxes' and that

'all concerned' should 'pay special attention to the handling of this class of traffic with the objective of avoiding any possible cause for damage'. Some years later, in October 1930, it was reported that Messrs Lyons & Co had complained that loose tea and confectionery was 'arriving at destination in an unsatisfactory condition which is said to be due to bad treatment in transit'. A further instruction, in December, brought the attention of staff to the 'large quantity of shrubs, plants in pots etc' that were now passing 'from various stations to all parts of the country', adding that special care was required in stowing such items.

While some loads, like fish and livestock, had of necessity to be moved rapidly, some of the miscellaneous traffic described above, carried in mixed goods services, could take rather longer to get reach its destination. During the 1920s and 1930s the GWR, responding to the growing threat of competition from road hauliers, which could deliver goods quickly and 'door-to-door', worked hard to increase the speed of all its goods trains. 'The acceleration of goods services has occupied a very important part in the freight development policy of the Great Western

ABOVE This view of the goods yard at Bodmin in 1925 illustrates the huge variety of goods carried on the railway. As well as three coal wagons and a horsebox, 'Mink' and various other covered vans can be seen.

TOP RIGHT A pannier tank heads a typical mixed goods, as operated all over the GWR network.

BOTTOM RIGHT Standing very close to the line, a family watch '28xx' 2-8-0 No 2828, built in 1907, thundering past at the head of a vacuum-fitted express goods.

Railway in recent years,' the company stated in 1936, claiming that the 'speed and regularity of services was a matter for justifiable pride'; furthermore it had introduced increasing numbers of fast freight services 'which in conjunction with the many supplementary and feeder services enable one-day transits to be afforded for general merchandise between all important towns'. These vacuum-braked trains could be run at passenger train speeds and enabled goods to be moved much quicker than previously.

TOP **An early design of GWR container being loaded by mobile crane onto one of the company's Thornycroft lorries. The photograph was taken at Paddington on 12 December 1927.**

ABOVE **This insulated container, photographed at Penzance in 1936, was loaded not with fish but with bulbs bound for Manor Farm at Marazion. In the background to its right can be seen a 'Bloater' fish wagon.**

Many of the fastest freight trains on the GWR ran between Paddington and Bristol, the West Country, South Wales and the Midlands. Large passenger locomotives, such as the 'Castles', were used, as were the nine Churchward '47xx' 2-8-0s, which were employed almost exclusively on these duties. Many of these high-speed trains were given names that reflected either their destination or the goods carried; the railway argued that this practice enhanced 'the mere duty to ensure prompt despatch and the elimination of all possible delays, and seems to place a personal responsibility upon each man on the entire run'. Thus the 3.55pm Birkenhead–Smithfield train was nicknamed the 'Meat' in recognition of the load being carried to market in the capital, while the 8.20pm from Kidderminster to Paddington was known as the 'Carpet', reflecting the principal trade of the Worcestershire town. Other names were clearly the result of railway wit, the 12.5am Worcester–Paddington 'Sauce' being among the better examples.

In 1929 the Great Western introduced a 'Registered Transit' service which enabled traders to send consignments that had guaranteed delivery times; a premium of 2s 6d was charged, and delivery was controlled from 'point to point' subject to 'fog and unavoidable risks', but, the GWR argued, the new system allowed traders to 'argue to a nicety the time at which their goods will be delivered to a customer'. What became known as the 'Green Arrow' network was subsequently adopted by the other 'Big Four' railways and proved very popular commercially; in 1935 alone the GWR dealt with more than 135,000 consignments, the company reporting the following year that the service was 'of inestimable value' to traders.

A further innovation aimed at speeding freight transport was the adoption of containers; company publicity described the container as 'in effect, an immense packing case into which goods may be packed at the sender's premises ... and conveyed throughout to the customer's door'. Road-rail containers came in various sizes and were used for various purposes, some being suitable for general merchandise and others for bulk items such as grain. There were also special ventilated containers, built to carry fresh meat and fish, and insulated varieties for chilled and frozen meat, fish and poultry. Containers were delivered empty to senders by GWR lorry and collected when filled; they were then loaded by crane onto wagons and sent by express train to their destination, from where another GWR road vehicle would deliver each container to its ultimate destination. Once a container was locked the keys would be forwarded direct to the customer, ensuring that load could not be tampered with *en route*. One particular type of container used by the GWR was provided for another service it offered. 'A household removal, even in the most favourable circumstances, may be troublesome,' the company noted in 1936, adding that any anxiety would disappear 'if the whole of the work is entrusted to the removal experts of the GWR'. The removal service was used by 'thousands of householders', a added advantage being, the company contended, the provision of reduced rail fares for all members of the household travelling from the old residence to the new. In addition to domestic removals the railway provided a commercial service for factory removals, dismantling and packing plant and equipment before moving it to new premises. A similar service was offered for farm removals, with staff tackling the additional task of moving livestock.

The collection and delivery of containers was possible only because of the sizeable fleet of road vehicles owned and operated by the GWR. 'Anything, anywhere, at any time' could

be conveyed, 'without exaggeration', the company claimed. The railway had always offered what it called 'town cartage', delivering goods to customers in urban areas, but it developed other services including 'Railhead Distribution', which involved the use of express cartage vehicles to deliver goods to major centres like Bristol, Birmingham, Cardiff, Swansea and Exeter by overnight express goods trains, ensuring 'next-day' delivery. Away from larger towns and cities it introduced the Country Lorry Service, which enabled merchandise, parcels and agricultural goods including milk to be delivered and collected from 'shops, farms and private residences' within 20 miles of more than 160 stations on the GWR system. The railway also built and maintained its own fleet of road vehicles for moving livestock to and from markets and carried all manner of other kinds of merchandise, including sand and gravel, building materials pipes and machinery. The road-transport department could also handle special and unusual loads, including industrial boilers and equipment, transformers and other bulky items, confirming its claim that it had 'developed its cartage business outside the traditional limits of railway operations' — a boast that could be extended to its entire goods operation.

ABOVE As a 'common carrier' the GWR was obliged to transport any load presented for despatch. Among the more unusual was this yacht, pictured aboard a 'Crocodile' wagon at Kingswear on 28 June 1937.

BELOW Away from the large towns and cities the GWR maintained numerous goods facilities of more modest scale. This small lock-up shed at Hemyock, on the Culm Valley line in Devon, was of corrugated-iron construction.

PART 2: SPRING

Away from the smoke and grime of the company's London terminus, as spring approached many GWR staff made use of the fresh air and better weather to begin the task of tending the gardens that many stations had. Although no precise date can be found for the establishment of the first station garden the Bristol & Exeter Railway is thought to have been the first railway company to set up a competition for the best-kept garden, in 1864. Less than a decade later the B&E had been absorbed by the Great Western, and the scheme was widened to encompass the whole network, beginning what became an annual tradition of an award by Great Western directors of a sum of money to be divided amongst those stations on the network that had prize-winning gardens.

A circular issued by the General Manager in March 1925 noted that prizes would be awarded to stations, taking account of the situation, soil and climate; the GWR was more fortunate than other 'Big Four' companies in that a large number of its stations were situated in the West Country, where the weather was normally mild, enabling more exotic plants to be cultivated.

BELOW The station gardens at Brislington, on the GWR line between Bristol and Radstock.

GWR management was, however, anxious that gardens should not be confined to attractive rural locations; an earlier circular, issued just before the Great War, had urged staff to establish gardens at stations where none was present, their establishment being considered a 'matter of importance', adding that it 'particularly desired to impress on members of staff in mining or manufacturing districts the desirability of establishing and maintaining gardens'. One writer has described the 1920s and 1930s as the zenith of the station garden, and certainly the standard of horticulture in both rural and urban locations was at its most imaginative and enthusiastic. A description of Kidlington station published in the *Great Western Railway Magazine* in 1927 noted that one platform featured a lawn inset with roses, and a border that included snapdragons, balsam, verbena and columbine; rockeries aside, the garden's main feature was a pergola that stretched along one side of the station and featured intertwined lavender, rambling roses and honeysuckle, while located under an arch at the end was a seat where passengers could 'wait for their trains and imagine themselves miles away from a railway'.

In addition to floral displays many stations, especially those with poorer soil, featured advertising in what was described as 'horticultural signwriting'. Messages, usually based on slogans from GWR publicity, were spelled out in white pebbles or even larger stones, with bedding plants providing a colourful background. Perhaps the most ingenious was that provided at Challow, Berkshire — 'Cheap Holidays Advertised London Lands-End or Wales'. No matter how attractive the displays at stations, the company expected a little more of award-winning locations; in 1925 the General Manager warned staff that no prize would be awarded 'unless the platforms, offices, waiting rooms, lavatories etc have been kept clean and tidy, and the work of the station performed in a satisfactory manner'. In 1928 the prize fund allocated by the GWR directors amounted to £400, this being shared between 221 stations; a further £26 was allocated for the 29 that also provided hanging baskets. Prizes of £5 were also awarded to a number of stations where the gardens were judged to have been particularly impressive; in 1928 these included locations all over the Great Western network, including St Devereux in Cornwall, Dinas Powis in South Wales, Yatton on the Bristol–Exeter main line and King's Sutton in the Midlands.

Another sign of improving weather and the promise of summer was the appearance of *Holiday Haunts*, the company's most important printed publication apart from its public timetables. Each edition took almost a year to produce, and while holidaymakers may have bought their copies in the springtime in anticipation of a forthcoming summer holiday, the work required to produce the next volume began almost as soon as the new edition was issued. The book always featured views illustrating the scenery and sights of the places served by the GWR, and

ABOVE In the West Country many station gardens featured exotic plants that could grow in the region's warmer, frost-free climate. This view of Lostwithiel, recorded in 1956, includes a rather bedraggled palm tree.
H. C. Casserley collection

photographers went out into the countryside soon after publication to complete the task of finding new views to include. The rule, noted Miss Maxwell Fraser in an article in the company magazine in 1930, was to try to avoid pictures with the 'allurement of holiday seasons', and wherever possible images with people in bathing costumes were excluded, as many of the places featured were as popular for winter breaks as for summer holidays.

Holiday Haunts also included a large amount of advertising for all sorts of accommodation, and much of the responsibility for collecting and canvassing for these advertisements fell to individual stationmasters. A circular issued by the Superintendent of the Line in January 1922 provides some insight into the whole process, confirming that canvassing for that year's issue of the book would be undertaken by Station Masters or 'responsible members of their staff'. As an incentive and to ensure 'the best possible results a commission of 10 per cent will be allowed to the Station staff of the receipts from all advertisements secured by them,' it continued. Canvassing was to start 'at once', urged the circular, with those who had taken advertisements in 1921 to be approached first, and every effort made to find new advertisers. *Holiday Haunts* was, however, an 'official publication' of the company, noted the Superintendent of the Line, and as a result all publicity material included therein could be considered to have its 'approval'; staff were therefore warned not to accept any advertisement of accommodation 'which the Company would not be in a position to recommend'. Quite how staff were to check the veracity of advertisers' claims was not explained in the circular!

With the canvassing work over, the advertisements could be compiled and the book assembled (complete with letterpress text on the various areas and resorts served by the railway),

ABOVE A 1939 advertisement for *Holiday Haunts*.

edited and finally proof-read. Once this process was complete *Holiday Haunts* was printed at the works of Butler & Tanner, close to the West of England main line at Frome, and by March the new publication was being featured in advertisements locally and nationally; on 14 March 1928 *The Times* featured a substantial advertisement that noted optimistically: 'A fine summer is expected: why not plan your holiday now?' The advertising copy continued: 'everyone begins to look forward to their summer holiday, but where to go is sometimes a problem. You probably need advice, most reliably found in *Holiday Haunts*.' The 1928 edition of the book, modestly described by the Great Western as 'the greatest of all holiday guides', contained 8,000 holiday addresses, 700 resorts 'fully described' and 400 illustrations and was available for 6d from GWR stations, town offices and booksellers and post-free from the Superintendent of the Line at Paddington.

The appearance in spring of *Holiday Haunts* and the impending Easter holiday period signalled the beginning of a sustained drive by the GWR to promote and develop its summer holiday business. In the 1920s and 1930s these efforts were increasingly matched by investment from councils, businesses, hotel owners and other accommodation providers, who spent large sums to attract holidaymakers to both seaside and inland resorts and attractions. Previewing the forthcoming holiday season in the spring of 1934, the company argued that the summer was 'likely to be one of the best experienced for many years', with increased optimism amongst the public due to a gradual return to normality after the Depression that had begun with the Wall Street Crash in 1929. The article summarised developments in holiday resorts all over the GWR system, including a new pavilion (costing in excess of £25,000) on the seafront at Aberystwyth and new swimming pools, golf courses and promenades at locations as varied as Barry, Bath, Penzance, Torquay and Weston-super-Mare, as well as a host of other facilities, such as cinemas, gardens and tennis courts. The article

ABOVE *Holiday Haunts* usually included scenic views recorded all over the GWR network by staff photographers. This one features the harbour at the Cornish fishing port of Looe.

also previewed the facilities the GWR was to offer in the coming months to encourage 'homeland holidays', arguing that 'Economy, convenience, and the absence of irritating restrictions are features characteristic of present-day railway service'.

By the 1930s there was a huge variety of special tickets available for holidaymakers, and, for ticket-office staff at stations all over the network, spring was a time to examine closely instructions sent from Paddington to ensure they were familiar with all the packages on offer. In the company magazine for March 1936 an article titled 'This Year's GWR Holiday Plans' reminded staff that the railway had been 'working ceaselessly' behind the scenes to ensure that holidaymakers had the best services for the forthcoming season. In the next few months, it noted that 'many of us, as railway folk, are going to be asked our advice on the subjects of holidays and travel' and that staff would be expected to know 'the broad outlines of what the company has to offer'.

With road competition becoming more and more of a problem the railway had little choice but to provide attractively priced tickets to maintain its business. The 'Summer Ticket', which cost a 'single fare and a third' for a return journey, had no restrictions and could be used on any day and on any train, with return possible within a month. The company argued that these tickets were 'amazingly cheap', boasting that 'the family man deserves something special and gets it', as children under three travelled free, and that even 'the biggest of big kiddies' under 14 years old travelled half-fare; the perambulator and cot were all carried free of charge, although 'the dog, who now has his holiday too, gets his return ticket at the single journey rate'.

The company also marketed seven-day 'Holiday Season Tickets' that allowed holidaymakers unlimited travel within particular geographical areas; General Instructions issued by the Superintendent of the Line in March 1938 asked 'all concerned' to note that Holiday Season Tickets would be available from 1 April to 31 October that year and went on to list in detail the 25 different areas for which these tickets were available, as well as the stations covered by each. The area designated as No 1 on the list covered West Cornwall and included the GWR stations at Penzance, St Ives, Helston, Newquay, Truro and Falmouth. A rather larger area was encompassed by the No 9 ticket, which covered a good part of Herefordshire and Gloucestershire in the Wye Valley and Forest of Dean and included stations such as Hereford, Monmouth, Tintern, Lydney, Usk and Abergavenny. Three further tourist season tickets were available for the Cotswolds and Shakespeare Country, while five others covered North, Mid and West Wales. For most areas the Third-class ticket cost just 10s 6d for the seven days, although for some reason season tickets for Dorset stations were 3s dearer. Two others that cost more also included boat travel on the River Dart as part of the package. By 1937 the company's timetable also offered seven-day holiday season tickets for passengers' bicycles and dogs; each bicycle ticket cost 5s, while dogs could have unlimited travel for 2s 6d. Perhaps anxious to prevent holiday tickets' being used by regular passengers in the summer months as a way of cutting the cost of their day-to-day travel, GWR publicity material was very clear about their purpose; holiday season tickets were issued to 'Visitors solely for holiday purposes', according to a 1925 handbill advertising services in Somerset and Dorset.

The cheapest form of holiday travel was, the company argued, the half-day excursion ticket; at about three miles per penny, fares were relatively cheap, and the GWR worked hard to attract not only individuals and families but also groups and parties of all types. 'Attractive country, riverside or seaside resorts, as well as places of interest are conveniently reached by rail from all parts of the Great Western railway system', boasted an advertisement in the 1930 *Holiday Haunts*, while four years

ABOVE A Thornycroft bus used by the GWR's publicity department, pictured at the less-than-scenic location of Swindon station. On the right can be seen a GWR poster promoting the natural brine baths at Droitwich.

later it was reported that by the end of March more than 2,500 trips from stations all over the network had already been organised for the coming season. Secretaries and organisers of works, school and church or chapel outings were encouraged to 'communicate early with any Great Western station-master' to book excursion tickets, and free savings cards were provided to enable organisers to pay by instalments before the trip. Reduced fares were available for parties as small as eight people, although for much larger groups better discounts were offered, along with free travel for the organiser.

While many groups already had a good idea of their excursion destination, the railway produced a booklet, 'Suggestions for Party Outings', which sought to help organisers 'arrive at a popular decision'. In addition to 'pleasure resorts' such as Barry and Weston-super-Mare, the 1936 publication listed inland locations, notably London, Oxford and Stratford-upon-Avon; also mentioned were 'industrial centres of interest' that included some of the biggest factories and industrial concerns on the GWR network. The railway began running excursions to its own workshops at Swindon in the 1920s and continued to promote these throughout the interwar period; a half-day excursion 'to the birthplace of the Cheltenham Flyer' from Bristol and other West Country locations included a tour of the works led by 'locomotive experts', noted a 1935 handbill, which added that books, jigsaw puzzles and prints of locomotives would be on sale on the train. Similar trips were also organised to Oxford, these including a tour of the colleges followed by a 'comprehensive' tour of the Morris Motors factory at Cowley; having seen 'cars in all stages of construction' excursionists could take tea in the

ABOVE A poster advertising one of a series of excursions run by the GWR to Oxford, featuring a tour of both the Morris factory and historic colleges in the city. *British Motor Industry Heritage Trust*

RIGHT The interior of one of the open carriages built by the GWR in April 1935 for excursion traffic.

Morris Club House and still have time for a brief walk around the city. Other industrial destinations included the famous 'Factory in a Garden' at Bournville, where visitors could view both the chocolate-production plant and the nearby garden village. Another popular attraction for GWR from Wales and the Midlands was Port Sunlight, advertised as the 'Largest Soap Factory in the World'.

Large numbers of people travelled to conferences, shows and religious, educational and musical events on specially priced tickets provided by the GWR, and the weekly General Instructions issued to staff were usually filled with detailed lists of reduced-fare packages of which the company's hard-pressed ticket clerks and station staff would need to be aware. Surviving records from the spring of 1930 reveal a huge variety of events; the circular issued on 14 March lists conferences held by the National Federation of Fruit & Potato Trades Association, the Baptist Laymen's Missionary Movement and the British Women's Temperance Association, along with another seven meetings. The following week reduced-fare facilities were available for another 14 events, including the Chemical Society's General Meeting & Annual Dinner, the National Union of Students' Universities Congress and the Bristol Eisteddfod. A rather more sombre but regular group of people offered cheap tickets during the 1920s and 1930s were ex-servicemen and their families. The British Legion and other organisations such as the Association of Ex-Civil Servants organised annual 'pilgrimages' to the battlefields of France and Belgium; a circular dated 8 April 1938 gave details of two such trips to Ypres and Arras, for which tickets at a much-reduced fare were provided for groups travelling to South Coast ports.

Yet another initiative to be noted by station staff involved 'Circular Tours' encompassing 'selected places of interest' on the GWR system; such tickets permitted the traveller a route that 'may be as diverse as desired, with stops of a day or more in special places of interest,' company publicity noted. In the main these tours were pre-arranged and timetabled by the company and could embrace travel in any part of England, Wales, Scotland or Ireland, but in 1934 the *Great Western Railway Magazine*

ABOVE **Happy excursionists pose for the camera at Reading station alongside 'Hall' 4-6-0 No 4937 *Lanelay Hall*.**

reported of an 'an enterprising feature' whereby itineraries could be set by holidaymakers themselves by prior arrangement. A circular issued by the GWR in 1938 reminded staff that applications of this type should be made by letter and forwarded to Paddington, where fares and arrangements could be investigated; travel could include 'rail, road, sea or air', and hotel accommodation could also be booked at the same time.

Among the holiday packages offered by the GWR were Land Cruises; described as 'personally conducted "all-expense" motor tours through England', these included First-class travel, hotel accommodation, meals, gratuities and admission to places of interest. The company's 1937 summer timetable offered four Land Cruises; three, to North Wales, Cornwall and Devon respectively, were six-day tours, while the fourth was a 13-day extravaganza that took in Bath, Cheddar, Weston-super-Mare, Exmoor, Dartmoor, Exeter and the Cornish Riviera. At other times the GWR ran Land Cruises to other areas, including 'Shakespeare Country', the Forest of Dean and the Wye Valley; these had been 'planned to provide for the maximum of sight-seeing without fatigue', noted an advertisement, which added that they 'could not be run under more comfortable conditions or at less cost'. Very popular, the Land Cruises were forerunners of the package tours that are so common today; they were 'definitely travel deluxe', asserted the company magazine, being 'organised in such a way as to leave the holidaymaker the sole and inevitable duty of enjoying himself'.

At the end of a long, cold winter the delights of summer were still some way off, and for travellers on the GWR Easter generally presented the first opportunity for a short break or day out; it was thus the railway's first busy weekend of the year, and although summer timetables were not yet in operation special schedules were introduced, as extra trains had to be provided during busy periods. Much depended upon the weather, which was not always kind at this time of year; in 1925 a memorandum issued by the Divisional Superintendent's Office at Bristol reported that it had been 'generally cold and wet'. Patronage had been 'good in view of conditions', it continued, but the rain must nevertheless have dampened the enthusiasm of travellers, for the level of traffic was recorded as being only two thirds of that seen the previous year. Only 10,500 passengers travelled to Weston-super-Mare, compared with 12,300 the year before, and trains to Clevedon and Severn Beach were also quieter, the numbers visiting Portishead being reduced by half. More positive was the news that long-distance excursions were busier than they had been a year previously; it was noted that 'traffic worked well', and the programme of trains provided meant that not as many emergency specials were required to cope with additional demand.

The Bristol Diaries for 1925 include minutes of a meeting held at Bristol to review the working of passenger trains for the whole Easter period that year, for, despite the best efforts of staff, some services had run very late. The 5.30 Paddington–Penzance of 7 April was described as being 'unsatisfactory', the train having reached its destination some 59 minutes late on account of time lost at Bristol, where delays were caused by the loading of large amounts of luggage for Taunton School, as well as fish traffic. Overcrowding was also a problem, and it was reported that on 9 April the Paddington–Cheltenham service arrived almost an hour late, largely because it consisted of 14 overcrowded coaches, which meant time was wasted at stations with shorter platforms, where the train had to move up several times to allow passengers to get off safely, although matters were also not helped by heavy congestion at Paddington.

Following Easter further strain was put on the GWR in 1925 by the need to provide special trains for thousands of football supporters attending the FA Cup Final at Wembley involving Cardiff City and Sheffield United on 25 April (this being, incidentally, the first since 1885 to feature a non-English team). To cope with demand the company ran 56 extra trains, two the previous night being followed by a resumption of services as early as 1.25am. While 18 of these, not surprisingly, originated from Cardiff itself, others ran from stations in the Valleys, including Treherbert, Blaina, Merthyr and Aberdare, as well as Newport and Bristol. Unfortunately the Cardiff supporters would not have enjoyed their journey home, their team having lost 1-0, but the successful transportation of so many people prompted the Superintendent of the Line to write to Divisional Superintendents following the game, congratulating them on their efforts and noting that 'the whole staff seem to have co-operated with the one desire to work the traffic in an efficient and satisfactory manner'.

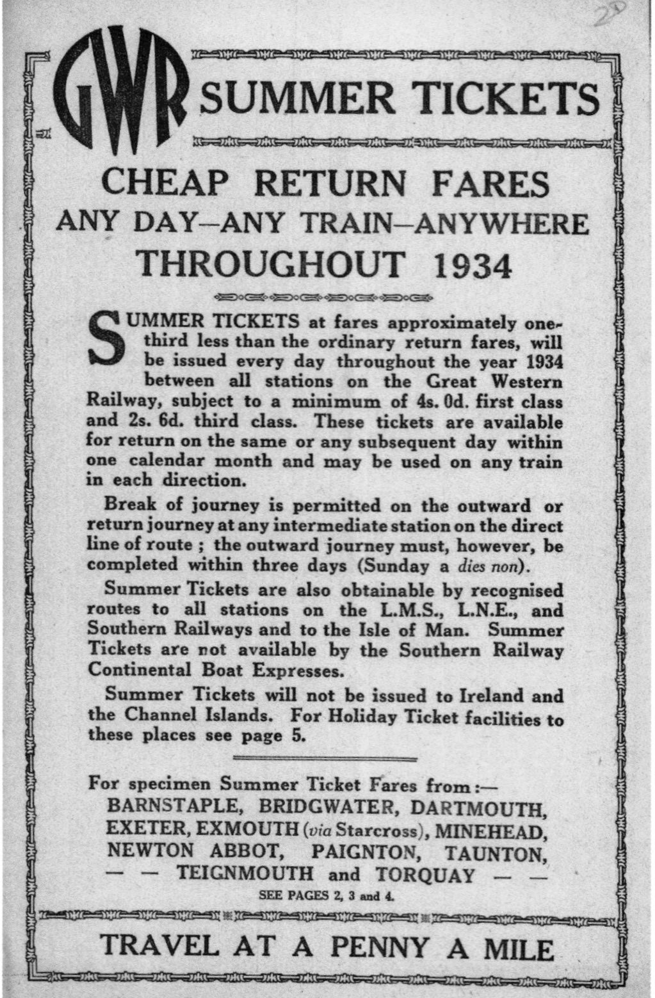

GWR SUMMER TICKETS

CHEAP RETURN FARES
ANY DAY–ANY TRAIN–ANYWHERE
THROUGHOUT 1934

SUMMER TICKETS at fares approximately one-third less than the ordinary return fares, will be issued every day throughout the year 1934 between all stations on the Great Western Railway, subject to a minimum of 4s. 0d. first class and 2s. 6d. third class. These tickets are available for return on the same or any subsequent day within one calendar month and may be used on any train in each direction.

Break of journey is permitted on the outward or return journey at any intermediate station on the direct line of route; the outward journey must, however, be completed within three days (Sunday a *dies non*).

Summer Tickets are also obtainable by recognised routes to all stations on the L.M.S., L.N.E., and Southern Railways and to the Isle of Man. Summer Tickets are not available by the Southern Railway Continental Boat Expresses.

Summer Tickets will not be issued to Ireland and the Channel Islands. For Holiday Ticket facilities to these places see page 5.

For specimen Summer Ticket Fares from:—
BARNSTAPLE, BRIDGWATER, DARTMOUTH, EXETER, EXMOUTH (*via* Starcross), MINEHEAD, NEWTON ABBOT, PAIGNTON, TAUNTON, — — TEIGNMOUTH and TORQUAY — —
SEE PAGES 2, 3 and 4.

TRAVEL AT A PENNY A MILE

ABOVE Bristol Temple Meads was an extremely busy place in the 1920s and 1930s — a situation complicated by the fact that it was run jointly with the LMS, one of whose delivery lorries can be seen in the background of this 1929 photograph.

LEFT 'Penny-a-mile' tickets were among the incentives offered by the GWR in the 1930s to encourage holidaymakers to travel by rail rather than road.

ABOVE **A quiet spell at Bristol Temple Meads, captured in 1936. By this date the station had undergone substantial modernisation as a result of Government assistance.**

Cardiff returned to Wembley in 1927 and on this occasion won the FA Cup, beating Arsenal. Once again the GWR rose to the occasion, transporting more than 21,000 passengers on 45 special trains. The company magazine reported that more than 4,000 packages of luggage and food were deposited in the cloakrooms at Paddington; demand for refreshments was so high that a temporary buffet was provided 'for the duration'. The Cup Final weekend followed a very busy Easter, the General Manager recording that holiday traffic was 'exceedingly heavy', many of the principal timetabled services being run as two or more separate trains on Maundy Thursday, 14 April. The railway ran an additional 47 trains, and demand was so high that the 'Cornish Riviera Limited' was run in four separate portions carrying more than 1,500 people in total. On that day excursion traffic was heavy all over the system, and a further 20 additional trains were run from Paddington to various locations, conveying more than 15,000 people. Away from the capital the railway ran all manner of other excursions at Easter, not all aimed at passengers wishing to travel to the seaside. A handbill issued by the company in 1929 gives details of an excursion run on Good Friday from Machynlleth, Aberdovey and other Cambrian Coast stations to Bala, the main attraction being the Good Friday Eisteddfod at nearby Llandderfel, a well-known event that had been held there since 1898.

In 1937 Easter was much earlier, the *Bristol Times & Mirror* reporting that the weather was 'chilly but with a fine display of March sunshine'. More than 16,000 people arrived at the Bristol Channel resort of Weston-super-Mare, more than 4,500 via the GWR; 'overcoats were not scorned,' the article concluded, trippers making the best of their break despite the cool temperature. The Easter holiday normally marked the start of better, warmer weather, and it was at around this time that another seasonal landmark was marked by staff at offices, stations and depots around the network. Circulars were issued by the Stores Department at Swindon asking for the updating of 'coal folders' detailing the number of grates, 'burning hours' and storage accommodation at each depot, signalbox and station, along with the amount of coal left following the winter; this would enable the Stores Department to estimate the amount of coal required for the following winter. 'It should be specially noted that supplies of coal received in the summer months are not intended for use before the 1st October,' the circular concluded.

With the approach of a new holiday season the GWR's publicity department was keen to attract custom from overseas, especially tourists from the USA, and produced promotional material aimed

LEFT **An unidentified 'Castle' 4-6-0 speeds a West of England express through one of the tunnels near Dawlish.**

BELOW LEFT **A postcard view of the GWR station at Plymouth Millbay.**

RIGHT **Unloading mailbags from the United States Lines' *George Washington* onto a GWR tender at Plymouth in April 1927.**

specifically at that market. Even before the Great War the company had published a booklet that claimed: 'The GWR is the line *par excellence* for visiting the many places of historic and other interest to Americans while in England.' As well as promoting tourist spots as Bath, Chester, Henley-on-Thames and Stratford-upon-Avon the booklet urged travellers from the USA to visit Stoke Poges, the birthplace of William Penn, founder of the state of Pennsylvania.

A later booklet, distributed by the company at the Baltimore & Ohio Railroad's centenary pageant in the autumn of 1927, noted that the GWR traversed 'the finest river, valley, mountain, woodland and pastoral scenery in the British Isles' and served 'many places linked with Anglo-American history and literature', offering 'unique attractions' to the tourist from the United States. The intending visitor must 'GO GREAT WESTERN', the booklet continued, arguing that England could offer the sightseer more than any other country, 'no matter what its size and location'. As well as the 'entrancing vista' that unfolded for the traveller heading west from Paddington to 'old Cornwall' the railway served locations 'from whence journeyed the progenitors of the Great American peoples', it concluded.

Much was made by the GWR of its role as a link between New York and London, something that could be traced back to the days of Isambard Kingdom Brunel and his first steamship, the *Great Western*. 'Gigantic liners and triumphs of railway engineering' had now brought the two cities within six days' journey of each other, the booklet noted. Between the two world wars Plymouth became the main gateway for overseas travellers and especially visitors from the United States. While ocean liners did call at the port in the winter months, the onset of better Atlantic weather and sea conditions in the spring naturally saw Plymouth handling more passenger and mail traffic. The company's operations at the port dated back to 1857, when it had set up the Plymouth Great Western Dock Co in association with the Bristol & Exeter and South Devon railways. Although some passengers had disembarked from transatlantic services to catch trains to London in the years that followed, it was not until the 1890s that the Great Western began to see the potential of the port and started running high-speed express trains from Plymouth to Paddington, carrying both passengers and mail in competition with the London & South Western Railway, which also had a dock at Plymouth. The intensive competition between the two railways came to a head in 1906, the race to speed passengers and 'Ocean Mails' to the capital culminating in tragedy when an LSWR express was derailed at Salisbury, killing 24 passengers and four railway staff. By 1911 the companies had formally agreed to end competition for Ocean Mail and passenger traffic, which in future would be handled by the Great Western.

The GWR docks at Millbay, while too small for large ships to disembark passengers directly, was located next to Plymouth Sound, a deep-water inlet that could handle the biggest ocean liners as they called eastbound from New York to Southampton. Passengers leaving liners at Plymouth would, noted GWR publicity, 'avoid the slower sea journey up the English Channel and the possibility of being delayed by sea fogs'. This was made possible by the railway's running high-speed services to the capital, these comprising both scheduled services and special non-stop trains. An article in the *Great Western Railway Magazine* in 1922 noted this, reporting that while the company had catered for shipping traffic at Plymouth for many years, increasing numbers of steamship companies were now using the port both outward and homeward and that special trains were run 'when the number of passengers landed justifies that course'. More than 11,000 passengers had disembarked from

ABOVE The East Quay at Plymouth in September 1924, with a schooner departing for the Cornish port of Fowey.

RIGHT This posed photograph of West Country flowers being harvested was used in GWR publicity in the interwar period.

287 ships at Plymouth the previous year, and in 1922 the port welcomed two new services, that of the French liner *Paris* and Cunard's *Mauretania*. When the *Paris* called at Plymouth in May of that year more than 1,300 bags of mail and parcels were unloaded, along with a large number of passengers. The special train run on that occasion took 4hr 20min to reach Paddington; special instructions issued to staff in January 1922 reinforced the importance attached to Ocean Mail trains, noting that 'all concerned are hereby directed to give special attention to their working'. This enhanced level of attention extended to sending telegraph messages to Paddington as trains passed Exeter and Bristol — and Westbury, if they used the West of England line via Castle Cary. The special instructions also advised that a Travelling Ticket Collector should work on all such specials 'where possible', and if this were not possible stations where the train was due to call were to be contacted by Plymouth once it had left with its load of passengers or mail.

The level of traffic handled at Plymouth grew steadily in the 1920s, and in 1930 the company had a record year, with 789 calls by liners, a figure that had increased by more than 40 over the

ABOVE **An undated photograph taken at the West Wharf at Plymouth. The dockers in the foreground are loading GWR vans with fresh strawberries.**

previous year. Recording this at the beginning of a new 'season' in April 1931, the company magazine noted that the total of 46,008 passengers landed the previous year was likely to be exceeded with the addition of two further liners, the *Majestic*, the largest British liner then afloat, and the *Olympic*, sister ship of the ill-fated *Titanic*. Until 1927 the way in which passengers and mail were unloaded at Plymouth had remained much the same for well over two decades. When an ocean liner arrived in Plymouth Sound one or more of the company's smaller tender vessels would be sent out to meet it and, after the mail and passengers had been loaded, would return to the dock, where a large contingent of dock labourers would then carry mail bags and luggage to the train, which was standing ready on the quayside. This process was incredibly labour-intensive, and it was reported that between 130 and 150 men could be required and that 'there were few occasions when fewer than 100 men sufficed for the operation'. The arrangements for passengers arriving at Plymouth were explained in the timetables issued twice-yearly by the company; 'Great Western staff will relieve passengers of all trouble in connection with their baggage,' noted the 1938 summer timetable, which further informed travellers that GWR porters would deal with the customs process, unpacking and repacking luggage where required before stowing it on waiting special trains after inspection.

At the beginning of the 1927 season a new electric conveyor belt was installed on the dock near the Princess Royal Pier, reducing labour costs by two thirds and considerably speeding up the unloading and loading process. The first ship to use the new facilities, the *American Merchant*, called at the port on 19 February, when 1,221 bags of letters and 239 bags of parcels from New York were unloaded 'with the utmost rapidity'. The new facilities also enabled the GWR to cope with increased levels of traffic. In July 1929 staff at Plymouth dealt with no fewer than five liners calling in a single day, handling more than 2,000 mail bags, in excess of 800 passengers and 150 boxes of special freight valued at over $1 million. That year, to cope with increased traffic, the Great Western had also provided a new tender vessel, the *Sir John Hawkins*, and two years later the company invested further at Plymouth, purchasing another passenger tender boat, the *Sir Richard Grenville*. This twin-propeller vessel could accommodate 800 passengers on the

RIGHT **This postcard view of the dock at Weymouth probably dates from the early 1920s. Crowds await the arrival of a GWR steamer at the landing stage as a train stands ready to welcome passengers arriving from the Channel Islands.**

BELOW **The *St Helier* arriving at Weymouth in summer of 1929. Another GWR vessel, probably the *St Julien*, is already docked at the quay.**

ABOVE Loading broccoli at Penzance. Various delivery vehicles are in use, not all of them supplied by the GWR.

short journey to and from Plymouth Docks, and its promenade deck was, the company reported, left as clear as possible to enable mails and motor cars to be 'stowed expeditiously'. It replaced an elderly vessel of the same name that had originally been built in for the GWR in 1891 and was also equipped with catering facilities to enable it to be used on pleasure trips along the coast of Devon and Cornwall in the summer months when not otherwise engaged on ferrying passengers to and fro from ocean liners.

Describing the port facilities at Plymouth in 1937 in the annual publication *GWR Docks*, produced for the company (as well as extolling its virtues as the 'Gateway into England from the Atlantic Ocean'), H. N. Appleby described the facilities at Trinity Pier, a jetty of 'solid construction' that handled extensive traffic from ports on the Continent in fruit and general goods. Reporting that a large proportion of the strawberries that were imported into Britain from France came through Plymouth, he noted that in 3 hours 50 minutes the port had been able to unload 22,932 packages of strawberries and peas from three steamships and load them into railway wagons for transport to London and the Midlands.

Whilst the bulk of the fruit and vegetables carried by the GWR were grown in England and Wales, in spring Plymouth and the railway's other South Coast port, Weymouth, handled large quantities of imported early produce such as peas, potatoes, strawberries, tomatoes and flowers, grown both in the Channel Islands and in France. In the case of Plymouth, produce was shipped via the port of Brest, in Normandy. Instructions issued by the company for the 1925 season described the traffic as 'peas in bags and baskets, strawberries packed in baskets and sieves (both in crates) and in boat-shaped boxes tied with strings'. The colour of the strings — red, white or blue — denoted the quality of the fruit, and the instructions to staff listed the various producers, warning checkers on the dockside to 'take great care' not to mix up bags, boxes and cases; it also made a special request to staff, reminding them that in order for it to reach customers in the best possible condition fruit needed to be 'very carefully handled'. The way in which produce was moved by the GWR from the port depended upon the size of the cargo; if the produce did not exceed four wagonloads it was forwarded by scheduled services such as the 12.0 train from Penzance to various destinations in South Wales and the 12.25pm from Penzance–Birmingham, which also provided connections with the LMS via Bristol and the LNER via Banbury.

Wherever possible, fruit and vegetables were loaded into wagons fitted with vacuum brakes, to enable them to be run in high-speed passenger trains; using this kind of rolling stock also meant that handling (and hence the risk of damage to produce) was kept to a minimum. When substantial quantities of fruit and vegetables were ready for despatch, special trains of five or more wagons were run as required. In 1925 this train was timetabled to leave Plymouth at 3.3pm; taking a circuitous route, it ran via Exeter and Bristol, through the Severn Tunnel to Pontypool Road and thence via Hereford and Shrewsbury, finally reaching Crewe just before midnight. The working instructions also reveal the ultimate destination of much of this fresh produce, as they record the order in which wagons were to be marshalled and where they were bound. The order for trains via the Severn Tunnel was: Liverpool, Yorkshire (Bradford, Halifax, Huddersfield, and Leeds), the LMS Lancashire & Yorkshire section (Stockport and Manchester), Wigan, Blackburn, Crewe. In many respects these special produce trains were treated like the fastest express services, and great efforts were made to ensure they ran to time and that the fresh fruit and vegetables arrived at their destination as quickly as possible. The working instructions required stationmasters along the route to keep an eye on their progress so that any shunting on the main line could be suspended to allow trains to pass without delay, and excursion and local stopping trains were to be shunted into passing loops to allow the fruit specials to overtake them.

As described earlier, the mild climate enjoyed by the Isles of Scilly and the Channel Islands had led to the development of a significant trade in cut flowers in the winter, and this continued well into the spring, along with further crops of fruit and vegetables. While produce from the Isles of Scilly Isles was handled at Penzance, Weymouth dealt with the bulk of traffic emanating from the Channel Islands. In his annual report for 1930 the Divisional Superintendent at Bristol, under whose management the port of Weymouth rested, was able to record that a tri-weekly sailing during the flower season had been provided, traffic being very heavy, to the point that 'the mail boat was also well loaded' with flowers. This business was followed by the importation of early new potatoes from the Channel Islands — a task shared with the Southern Railway, which also operated steamship services to and from the mainland; the shipment of potatoes was a source of valuable income to the railway, and in May and June 1929 the GWR handled almost 15,000 tons of this traffic, with a value of more than £30,000. Although some potatoes were moved as part of regular goods services (as was the case with strawberry traffic from Plymouth) special trains were also provided, although these ran only run if there were at least 15 wagons. A special notice produced by the GWR some years earlier explained that 'trains conveying perishable traffic from the Channel Islands should maintain their schedules,' adding that they must start punctually and that 'all concerned are requested to give the workings special attention'. Not surprisingly, the level of business from the Channel Islands depended heavily upon the weather and other natural hazards to crops, such as disease and pest infestation.

Much of the fresh Channel Islands produce handled by the GWR at Weymouth was carried by two cargo ships brought into service by the company in 1925. Following the Grouping in 1923 the directors

LEFT The GWR was acutely aware that damage to fragile loads like spring produce was costly in terms of insurance claims from farmers and could lead to producers' moving to road transport. Innovations such as these wooden dividers, which prevented loads from shifting in transit, were introduced as a result.

ABOVE Unloading broccoli and other vegetables at Paddington Goods Depot. The number of women in evidence suggests that the photograph was taken during World War 2.

and management of the railway had visited the South Coast and travelled to the islands, making an inspection of both the ships and associated dock facilities. It was clear that the rather elderly cargo ships, *Gazelle* and *Lynx*, used on Channel Island services were in need of replacement, both dating from 1889. Anxious to ensure that it could continue to support the fruit and vegetable trade, the GWR in 1925 placed in service two new 776-ton cargo steamers, *Roebuck* and *Sambur*. To promote this new investment it organised two special cruises in May of that year, the first for prominent people in Weymouth, including the Mayor, aldermen, councillors, Corporation officials, traders and 'influential people', along with representatives of businesses in the South West of England and the press. Presided over by General Manager Sir Felix Pole, it was followed some days later by a trip around Jersey from St Helier for dignitaries from the Channel Islands, including the Lieutenant Governor. These public-relations events generated good coverage in regional newspapers, providing a welcome boost to the advertisements and publicity produced by the GWR at the beginning of every season, and, with the promise of better weather, the company could look forward to a busy summer.

Besides handling fruit, vegetables and flowers imported from the Channel Isles and the Continent the railway dealt with large tonnages of home-grown early produce. The crop most identified with the GWR, especially in Cornwall, was broccoli, which was ideal for the mild climate enjoyed by the Royal Duchy and became increasingly popular with the British public in the 1920s and 1930s. Broccoli (in common with other perishable produce) had been carried by rail since the opening of the West Cornwall Railway in 1859, and within 20 years more than 5,000 tons was being transported to London and other urban centres. This figure grew steadily, trebling by 1900, and continuing increases in demand meant that by 1932 the GWR was handling 26,000 tons — a total that five years later had risen to nearly 36,000 tons.

The efficient service provided by the GWR 'proved of inestimable benefit to the development of the broccoli traffic', the company boasted in 1933, supporting the efforts of Cornish

growers who had introduced new varieties of the vegetable in the late 1920s and improved packing methods considerably. It was, however, left to the GWR to ensure that the harvested crops were loaded promptly and then transported as quickly as possible to market. Special arrangements were made during the season for the company's Country Lorry fleet to collect the broccoli for despatch from farmers, delivering it to more than 20 stations on the Cornish main line and the St Ives, Helston, Falmouth and Newquay branches. At locations such as Gwinear Road, Marazion, Ponsandane and St Erth special loading banks were provided, although elsewhere wagons were loaded in ordinary sidings. Broccoli, delivered to stations in wooden crates, was normally transported by rail in cattle wagons, the design of which allowed plenty of ventilation to ensure that produce arrived fresh at market. Owing to the seasonal nature of the traffic, such vehicles were often drafted in from elsewhere for the duration of the harvest.

Loaded broccoli wagons were normally brought in smaller numbers from the various Cornish branch lines (or local stations on the main line) to assembly points such as Marazion or Penzance, where they would be marshalled into larger special trains. The perishable nature of the load meant that special trains were treated as vacuum-braked expresses; in April 1932 the railway ran 230 broccoli specials to all parts of Britain, including Bristol, Cardiff, Birmingham, Manchester and London, 12 trains being despatched on one day alone, three of them running direct to London. Three years later, in January 1935, the company ran 73 special trains from the Penzance area in a single week; larger 4-6-0 locomotives, including 'Granges', 'Halls' and, in BR days, even 'Castles', were used on broccoli specials, although by the late 1940s road competition had severely reduced the quantity of vegetables being moved by rail. By the 1959/60 season (the last when steam locomotives were used) only seven specials were required — two for London, two for South Wales and three for the Midlands.

Surviving company records such as the Bristol Diaries contain numerous excerpts from the *Times & Mirror*, which reported on the fortunes of West Country holiday resorts and the railways that served them. The last bank holiday before the summer

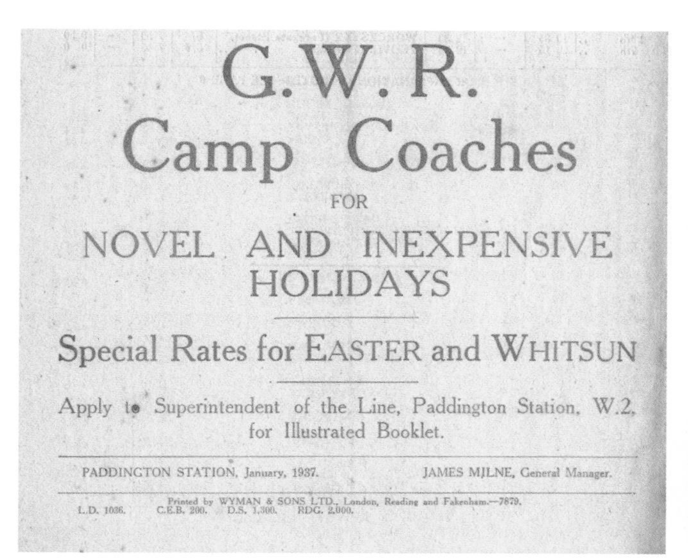
G.W.R.

Camp Coaches

FOR

NOVEL AND INEXPENSIVE HOLIDAYS

Special Rates for EASTER and WHITSUN

Apply to Superintendent of the Line, Paddington Station, W.2, for Illustrated Booklet.

PADDINGTON STATION, January, 1937. JAMES MILNE, General Manager.

Printed by WYMAN & SONS LTD., London, Reading and Fakenham.—7879.
L.D. 1036. C.E.B. 200. D.S. 1,300. RDG. 2,000.

ABOVE The cooler weather at Easter and Whitsun probably made Camping Coaches a rather less attractive proposition to holidaymakers, prompting the GWR to include this advertisement in a 1937 excursion booklet.

RIGHT A final scenic photograph commissioned by the GWR for publicity purposes, this time featuring 'A Cornish Garden' in March 1924.

LEFT Trippers on the quay and aboard the paddle-steamer *Compton Castle* at the Devon port of Dartmouth. In the middle distance can be seen the GWR ferry *Mew* waiting to cross the Dart to reach the railway station at Kingswear.

proper was Whitsun, and although the holiday period was shorter than that of Easter it was usually a busy time for the GWR. An article from 1930 reported that there had been record crowds at resorts; 'Parked trains poured from the Bristol stations,' while, in a sign of what was to come, 'endless streams of motor coaches travelled on arterial roads'. Despite the onset of road competition all records were broken that year by Whitsun traffic on the GWR, more than 80,000 people booking tickets at Bristol Temple Meads alone. As usual, Weston-super-Mare was the most popular location for trippers, some 27,000 passengers being carried there, followed by Weymouth (9,000) and Severn Beach (6,000).

Newspaper cuttings from 17 May 1937 describe another busy Whitsun bank holiday for the GWR. The *Western Daily Press* reported that it was 'summer frock and flannel suit weather', and the *Bristol Evening Post*, besides noting that it had been the finest day of the year so far and a very busy day for the resorts, described the introduction of public-address loudspeakers on the platforms at Weston-super-Mare. The system had been provided to keep 'home-going holidaymakers' informed of platform changes, trains and times, the report continued, with between 40 and 50 excursions arriving there during the day, the provision of clear announcements for weary excursionists at the end of a long day would doubtless have been very welcome. Whitsun was also seen by the GWR as an opportunity to promote the forthcoming summer holiday period; it advertised a number of excursions each year, and a 1936 handbill for a non-stop 'Restaurant Car Half Day Excursion' from Paddington to Weston-super-Mare on Whit Sunday assured prospective travellers that the outing afforded 'an excellent opportunity of securing accommodation' for their summer holidays.

FROM COW TO CORNFLAKE

In 1925 a publicity pamphlet issued by the GWR argued that families should have 'no difficulty' in obtaining regular supplies of food 'fresh from the dairy, the farmyard, or the garden', while the fact that the railway traversed counties 'noted for the richness of their agriculture ... is a sufficient guarantee that the produce will be of the first-class quality'. The pamphlet also included an exhaustive list of charges for the conveyance of what the company called 'perishable' traffic, including butter, cream, cheese, eggs, fruit and vegetables, honey, flowers, game and poultry, as well as a list of farmers and producers operating in areas served by the GWR. Contrasting with the situation today, when fruit, vegetables and produce of all kinds are available to consumers all year round through imports from overseas, between the wars many foodstuffs were still seasonal, and the GWR's goods department worked hard to ensure that harvested crops were collected and moved as quickly as possible. In the case of milk, however, the railway handled this vital traffic every day, all year round.

Railways were ultimately to revolutionise the way in which milk was carried and distributed in Great Britain, and although from the 1830s railway companies like the Liverpool & Manchester carried milk from the country into urban areas, for much of the 19th century large numbers of cows were still kept in towns and cities — or in the countryside close by — to supply milk for the urban population; one estimate noted that in 1865 more than 40,000 cows were kept in London alone. The milk that was brought in by railways could be moved relatively quickly from rural areas over long distances, but it was still not as fresh as that produced locally. However, following an outbreak of cattle plague in London in the 1870s the way in which milk was handled changed dramatically; new, larger companies, such as United

ABOVE Devon dairy cattle await loading as part of a farm removal on 29 September 1936.

LEFT A lengthy coal train hauled by a '28xx' 2-8-0 trundles through Little Somerford station, on the South Wales Direct line, in June 1932.

Dairies and the Express Dairy, replaced smaller local farm operations and provided milk to customers supplied from numerous dairy herds in rural areas that were often many miles from urban centres, and to satisfy the increasing demand for milk from cities further large areas of land were developed as pasture for dairy herds and meat production.

Depots and processing plants were created, notably the first major milk factory built by the Anglo-Swiss Condensed Milk Co, at Chippenham in 1873. In 1896 seven companies combined to form Wilts United Dairies; by this time the process of transporting milk from farm to dairy and on to the customer was being undertaken almost entirely by rail. By 1910 it was recorded that 96% of the milk consumed in the capital had arrived by train. Of the 'Big Four' railway companies that held sway from 1923 the GWR that carried by far the most milk, dominating the business in London and transporting almost 250,000 gallons into the city every day. Milk was brought to the capital from a number of locations, most within relatively easy reach of the capital, including Oxfordshire, Wiltshire, Gloucestershire, Somerset and Dorset. Elsewhere on the network the railway supplied Birmingham and adjacent centres areas such as Wolverhampton with milk from rural Shropshire, Warwickshire and Worcestershire. In South Wales urban centres like Cardiff and Swansea and the densely populated Valleys were supplied with milk from West Wales and Somerset. In the early 1920s milk from locations such as Neyland, Whitland, St Clears and Camarthen was moved on the 6.50pm from Neyland, which called at Swansea and Cardiff as well as supplying stations on the lines of the old Taff Vale and Rhymney companies.

In the years immediately after the Great War the way milk was carried on the Great Western was still much the same as it had been since the late-Victorian era; it was transported in galvanised metal milk churns delivered by farmers to country stations and loaded onto fast passenger services or special milk trains, numbers varying according to location. Station staff needed to be fit and strong to handle the loaded churns, for the older design of conical churn contained up to 17 gallons of milk, and even the newer cylindrical churn introduced in the 1930s could hold 10 gallons. To move them safely most porters tilted the churns onto one side and rolled them along the platform before loading them onto milk vans.

At smaller country stations the daily routine was usually very similar; at Little Somerford in Wiltshire a milk train called every morning to collect full churns, continuing to Badminton and stopping at all stations thence to Wootton Bassett, where the milk vans were added to those from other locations to form a longer train for London. In the 1920s more than two dozen farmers used Little Somerford station for dealing with their milk, the company charging them on a monthly basis; a sliding scale was applied depending upon distance, varying from less than 1d per gallon for journeys of up to 20 miles to more than 2d per gallon for those exceeding 150 miles. Even on a relatively minor line, such as the 5-mile Swindon–Highworth branch, dairy farms were an important source of traffic; a 1925 inspection of the line by the Bristol Divisional Superintendent revealed that 293 churns were conveyed daily in eight wagons from the branch's four stations, including 65 from the tiny halt at Hannington.

The GWR was keen to argue that it provided a good deal for farmers, noting in 1925 that its rates should be 'of assistance to farmers and others who have already found a market for milk in the Metropolis and in other large centres of population'. As competition from road hauliers increased, however, the railway reduced its rates where relatively large quantities of milk in churns was moved, offering 15% discount to farmers sending more than 1,000 gallons every year and 20% if this figure doubled

BELOW Empty milk churns being unloaded from a motor lorry at Highbridge station in 1928. The name of the station can clearly be seen on plates affixed to some of the churns.

ABOVE **A misty view of the west end of Paddington station, recorded just after the Great War. On the right empty milk churns await return to West Country farms.**

to 2,000 gallons. Not all farmers were prompt in paying their account, and at Little Somerford the porter, Len Hillman, was often sent out on his bicycle to collect overdue charges.

Much of the milk handled at Little Somerford and other rural stations ended up in London. The *Great Western Railway Magazine* reported in 1923 that the company was running around 60 special milk trains each weekday and 63 on Sundays; on many rural branch lines milk trains were the only services of any kind to run on Sundays, a result of both Sabbatarian demands and economic necessity on the part of the company. It was also noted that in 1922 the Great Western had carried over 75 million gallons of milk, the writer estimating that this enormous quantity amounted to the equivalent of around 64,000 special milk vans.

An important step forward in the efficient transportation of milk by rail had been the introduction of special rolling stock that could carry it without too much jolting and, importantly, keep it as cool as possible, especially in the summer months. On the GWR churns were carried in the guard's compartment of ordinary passenger trains when there were relatively few to handle at a station, but in general milk traffic was transported in six-wheeled or bogie wagons identified by the company's own telegraphic name of 'Siphon'. A number of variations of these vehicles were produced over the years, but they shared basic characteristics. Most 'Siphon' bodies when constructed were mounted on refurbished carriage chassis, which not only made economic sense but also ensured that they could be attached to the rear of scheduled passenger train services and run at high speeds or marshalled together in special express milk trains. As a result the GWR always classified them as passenger rather than goods stock.

The first 75 'Siphons', built at Swindon in the 1870s, were actually four-wheeled vehicles and were of all-wood construction (including the underframe) and fitted with 3ft 6in Mansell coach wheels with wooden centres. Just 18ft long, they were nevertheless capable of holding the larger 17-gallon churns stacked two deep.

ABOVE A typical 1920s milk train headed by a 'Hall' 4-6-0, the milk being transported in a variety of six-wheeled and bogie 'Siphon' vans.

These wagons had been withdrawn from service by the outbreak of the Great War, replaced by the 'Siphon C' design introduced in 1906 and the larger 'Siphon E' eight years later. These six-wheeled wagons were of an open boarded design, some with slatted ends. Later variations were taller, with a higher roofline and six double doors; a number were also fitted with end doors and a drop flap allowing milk churns to be loaded from a bay platform. This design was used extensively until the 1930s, by which time train speeds had increased significantly, and they were no longer suitable. By then larger 50ft bogie 'Siphon G' vehicles were in use, 150 having been constructed in six lots between 1913 and 1927. Later examples had gangways and electric light and could also be used for other loads when not in use for milk traffic. As well as proving practical for carrying parcels and general goods they were used to transport racing pigeons; although these remained in their baskets for the duration of the journey to their point of release, the vans would doubtless have required a thorough disinfecting afterwards!

In view of the need to keep milk as cool as possible it will perhaps be surprising to the reader that these wagons were not refrigerated; although the wooden-bodied 'Siphon' design included ventilation louvres to allow cooling air to circulate around the churns it was not until the 1930s that the railway began experimenting with chilling equipment, this being done at the behest of dairy companies wishing to improve the quality of milk arriving at depots. The final design produced, the 'Siphon J', embodied the more sophisticated idea of an insulated vehicle fitted with ice boxes to keep temperatures down. Characterised by the vertical planking (rather than louvres) on its sides, the 50ft bogie van had special sealed doors and was fitted with electric lighting so that no heat was generated inside the van; inside it could accommodate four of the old 17gal churns abreast. Eight new vehicles were built at Swindon in 1930, a further 27 following a year later, the number of wagons built being more modest than hitherto because the company had begun using tank wagons to carry milk. However, the changeover from churns to tanker-borne traffic took some years to complete, and many farms with smaller dairy herds continued to provided milk in churns, many of which remained in railway use until after World War 2.

By the 1920s the Great Western had a large fleet of vehicles retained exclusively for milk traffic, the company noting that on a typical day almost 7,500 churns of milk were delivered to London depots in 258 wagons, along with a further 626 churns carried in the guard's vans of passenger trains. To cope with the huge

ABOVE A six-wheel 'Low Siphon' milk van at Banbury, its slatted sides clearly revealing the churns inside.

BELOW The prototype 'Siphon G' bogie van, photographed at Swindon Works in 1923.

ABOVE **Recorded in 1923, this view of the west end of Platform 1 at Paddington features not only 'Star' 4-6-0 No 4061 *Glastonbury Abbey* but also large numbers of empty milk churns awaiting return — hardly the most attractive scene for passengers.**

volume of traffic at Paddington the GWR had steadily improved its facilities there, and when the decision was taken just before World War 1 to expand the Brunel terminus by adding a further roof span the opportunity was also taken to construct a new milk platform in the new part of the station, easing congestion on the existing platforms. The height of the new Platform 12 varied from 3ft at the west end of the station, suitable for normal carriages, to 3ft 9in at the east end in the milk section, allowing milk churns to be rolled straight out of wagons or carriages without being lifted and thus reducing the amount of jolting and shaking suffered by the milk, as well as making life rather easier for staff who manhandled the churns on a daily basis. Care was also taken to ensure that road access to the new platform was at a level that permitted milk churns to be loaded straight from the platform into wagons or lorries without additional lifting, and special non-slip road surfacing was included to help horses (which were still used in great numbers in the 1920s) to haul delivery wagons.

It was noted that a 'special staff of experienced men' was provided for dealing with milk traffic at Paddington, where facilities ensured that 'so far as handling is concerned, there can be little fault to find'. Although milk trains were scheduled to arrive throughout the day the busiest time for the men employed there was in the small hours of the night. It is not difficult to imagine that the sheer numbers of churns being handled must have generated a great deal of noise. The company had regularly to deal with complaints from people living in the vicinity of the station, and as early as 1887 the residents of Eastbourne Terrace wrote to the directors of the GWR, complaining of 'annoyance and injury' caused by the unloading of milk at night, 'with all its attendant shouting and bad language'. The situation had, they contended, 'assumed a very serious aspect'; unfortunately the company's response is not recorded, but staff were doubtless requested to temper their language in future. The difficulty of manhandling large milk churns quietly remained an issue; in the 1920s the *Great Western Railway Magazine* reported on the invention of the 'Silent Milk Churn', with a rubber tyre added to the base. This innovation would, it was hoped, 'make milk churn rattle out of date' and also reduce wear and tear on station platforms and lorry floors, yet it seems not to have been adopted to any great extent.

As already noted, much of the milk was brought to the capital in special express services, and to ensure that the whole process continued to work as smoothly as possible similar trains were required to return empty churns from dairies to their home stations. As the GWR was keen to emphasise in its publicity, no charge was made for the return of churns, which could also be returned during the day on a variety of normal trains. On arrival they had to be laboriously manhandled by station staff from down to up platforms, ready for collection by farmers. In view of the hundreds of churns being transported daily it was inevitable that there would be damage and losses, and General Instructions issued to staff in the 1920s and 1930s make numerous references to lost churns. As late as August 1939 a circular asked staff to make a thorough search for a 4gal churn branded 'Duffett, Bridgwater', which had been forwarded full from Bridgwater to the Canton Dairy Co in Cardiff and was now missing. 'The churn is said to have been returned empty from Cardiff,' it was noted, but had not arrived back at its home station.

A recurring theme in the history of the GWR in the years between the two world wars is the struggle by its management to modernise its facilities and services and persuade customers, staff and most importantly its shareholders and directors to support such new measures. The movement of milk churns already outlined, while an enormous undertaking, was also highly

BELOW A further view of the jumble of milk churns on Paddington's Platform 1, with a porter struggling to wheel a trolley through the chaos.

inefficient and labour-intensive; in addition it was increasingly inconvenient to farmers, who had to deliver churns to stations and collect the empties every day and who complained of their milk being spoiled by rough shunting and also of its theft during the journey. Road hauliers were quick to spot an opportunity, and the introduction from 1918 of tanker lorries meant that milk could be collected directly from farms with much less difficulty, reducing costs and pilferage and speeding the whole process. The GWR felt the impact of this competition keenly but was initially not quick to respond; headed 'No More Churns', a December 1925 article in the *Daily Express* claimed that 'the rattling of milk churns at railway junctions and little wayside stations will soon be heard no longer'. The correspondent reported that 'the morning milk' was now being sent by road from dairies and farms in 'immense glass tanks' holding more than 1,200 gallons, one of the main advantages being that milk was not exposed to the air and thus had less chance of being contaminated. Noting that Britain had been slow to address the problem of transporting milk, the manager of a dairy plant interviewed for the article was quoted as saying that 'the railway companies would not supply refrigerating vans, so we have solved the problem ourselves'. Milk that previously took 36 hours to get to its destination in summer could now arrive in half that time, he concluded.

The railway continued to lose business to road competition, but in 1927 the dairy industry and the main-line railway companies finally made a significant change in the way milk was handled, with the introduction of milk-tank wagons. These consisted of glass-lined tanks, which remained in the ownership of individual dairy companies or milk producers, mounted on a chassis built and owned by the GWR. With a capacity of 3,000 gallons, each milk tank could carry the equivalent of two six-wheeled 'Siphon' vehicles fully loaded with churns. The early four-wheel wagons featured a short wheelbase and were not a success; not permitted to run in trains at speeds above 60mph, they were replaced in 1932 by a longer-wheelbase six-wheel design that would remained standard until the 1960s.

The new tankers were part of a new, more integrated system for transporting milk in bulk by rail. A writer in the *Great Western*

BELOW Comprising a varied selection of vehicles, a milk train stands at Paddington on 13 July 1923, having arrived behind 'Badminton' 4-4-0 No 4119 *Wynnstay*.

Railway Magazine outlined what he called the 'Cow to Consumer' process, which became commonplace after 1927: having been taken from the cow, milk was poured untreated into sterilised churns (later direct into a tanker) ready for the first stage of their journey by road to one of the larger concentration depots or processing plants that had been established around the country; on the GWR these included the plants at Maiden Newton in Dorset, Yetminster in Somerset, Whitland in Pembrokeshire and Wootton Bassett in Wiltshire. Once delivered, milk was cooled and then loaded into rail tank wagons for despatch to urban dairies. Quicker and more hygienic than using churns throughout, as well as far less labour-intensive, this new operation signalled the beginning of a regular bulk milk service on the GWR, the company offering companies like United Dairies and Nestlé a 30% discount for the transport of milk in 3,000gal tanks. Tanker trains began running between the United Dairies plant at Wootton Bassett and its Mitre Bridge facility at Willesden in London in October 1927, and a month later it was recorded that more than 200,000 gallons had already been carried by these services. In 1931 the annual report produced by the Divisional Superintendent at Bristol recorded that 2,960,240 gallons of milk had been transported from Wootton Bassett to Mitre Bridge, an increase of almost 64,000 on 1930, although total income from this business, at £11,432, was nevertheless modest.

ABOVE Milk churns being loaded into a 'Siphon' wagon from a Milnes-Daimler lorry in 1936.

Further processing plants were constructed in the early 1930s at locations such as Whitland and Camarthen, and following completion of the Whitland facility a regular afternoon milk train was introduced which ran to United Dairies' Wootton Bassett facility and thence to Paddington. By 1935 the daily service was scheduled to leave Whitland at 2.50pm, with milk tanks bound for depots at Paddington, South Lambeth and Wood Lane, where a new large processing plant had been built in 1935 on land leased to United Dairies by the GWR. Recording the opening of the latter facility, the company argued that, besides being the largest, it was 'certainly the most up-to-date milk depot in the world'. Provided with what the company called 'adequate' sidings to meet traffic requirements, the depot had a reception platform

ABOVE **In an attempt to make life easier for staff loading and unloading heavy milk churns the GWR experimented with the use of this lever apparatus.**

that was 360ft long and nearly 30ft wide. Sixteen tank wagons and a further 1,000 churns were delivered daily to the depot, described by the company as 'one of the marvels of the milk industry'. Three years later tank wagons were being forwarded to other plants in and around the capital, notably at Mitre Bridge, Stewarts Lane and East Croydon.

The rare survival of a guard's journal report for a milk-train run from Whitland just after the end of World War 2, in November 1945, provides an interesting insight into the scale and nature of the service. The train consisted of 13 six-wheeled milk tank wagons and a 'Siphon' van, the latter running only as far Cardiff with its load of churns. The wagons came from all four main-line companies, the tanks being owned by United Dairies and the Milk Marketing Board. The six-wheeled wagons were extremely heavy when full, each weighing almost 28 tons, and as a result the train had a load of over 400 tons. Most milk trains of this type were therefore hauled by larger passenger locomotives, and while in the interwar years this might mean a 'Saint', 'Star' or 'Hall' the train run on 1 November 1945 had as its motive power 'Castle' No 5079 *Lysander*; Adrian Vaughan records that on occasion even a 'King' would be used on this service. Having left Whitland at 3.50pm, the train reached its destination at Southall in just under 8 hours, with stops at St Clears, Camarthen, Llanelly, Felin Fran, Ely and Cardiff, from there the train ran non-stop as far as Wootton Bassett, also calling at Swindon (to change crew) before resuming its journey to the capital. By the mid-1930s the Whitland milk train was one of almost a dozen scheduled services being run to the capital on weekdays from locations including Chippenham, Swindon, Oxford, Reading and as far away as Weymouth. Additional trains were also run from other stations to processing plants where tankers were shunted into larger trains bound for the capital, one such being the 5.40am Westbury–Wootton Bassett service.

Despite the progress made by the company in the running of bulk milk tanker trains, road competition continued to make inroads into the business, the Divisional Superintendent at Bristol noting in 1931 that a decrease in the quantity of milk transported by rail could be attributed to the 'diversion of milk to the road in heavy quantities'. Such diversions could have dramatic consequences; at Little Somerford milk traffic ceased entirely in December 1932, the number of churns handled having dropped from 32,485 in 1930 to just over 7,000 two years later, as a result of farmers' adoption of road haulage. The station was also the junction for the nearby Malmesbury branch, which had also seen a slump in its milk traffic after 1931. This was the last year in which milk was a major source of traffic on the line, as the dairy in Malmesbury, which hitherto had sent its entire output by rail, contributing significantly to an annual total exceeding 71,000 churns, now switched to the use of road tankers, leaving only a few farmers along the branch to provide milk for transport by the GWR; the service would be withdrawn altogether in 1938.

Adrian Vaughan records that from 1921 Traffic Superintendents had been suggesting to senior management that the GWR should run its own road-tanker service to collect milk from farmers but that the directors had been reluctant to sanction the necessary expenditure. In 1925, however, in an effort to combat the effects of road competition, the company did at least begin to develop further its Country Lorry Service — a move intended to support the development of traffic at rural stations by collecting and delivering goods and parcels. Introduced as early as 1908 in Cornwall and West Wales, the service had not initially been a great success, but after the war it was reintroduced and improved, subsequently being expanded to include the handling of milk traffic. Lorries so engaged ran daily to a strict timetable, the route being arranged to ensure that milk collected from scattered and, in many cases, remote farms would reach the station in good time to be loaded

BELOW A photograph taken before the Great War of a GWR milk depot in West London. The depot is not yet finished; besides the builders' rubble yet to be cleared, an unfinished fence can be seen in the distance.

onto a train. Station staff were sent out to ensure that GWR lorries could reach farms via narrow country lanes and that gateways and entrances were large enough for lorries to gain access to farmyards; where this was not possible milk churns would be left for collection on platforms constructed at the roadside.

Company publicity material noted that the use of lorry services by farmers would 'release their lorries, horses and carts for more important work', reminding them that one GWR lorry carrying milk could replace four or more of the farmer's horse-drawn carts or motor lorries; these larger railway vehicles would, it argued, also reduce wear and tear on roads in rural areas. The cartage of milk was, noted the *Guide to Economical Transport*, a regular feature, and for the conveyance of 'reasonable quantities' over a distance of up to 5 miles a rate of 1s 2d per gallon (including return of empty churns) would be charged.

In 1932 the GWR's road-transport department took over a major contract to collect and deliver milk to a concentration depot erected by Nestlé in the station yard at Lostwithiel in Cornwall. The dairy company had contracts with around 600 farmers in the county to provide up to 7,000 gallons of milk, every day of the week, and the collection of this enormous quantity over a vast area of rural Cornwall proved a considerable challenge, prompting the GWR to step in to maintain the contract. In all there were 24 separate lorry routes, worked by a fleet of (mostly) 2-ton lorries based at 10 locations including Lostwithiel. Some idea of the scale of the operation can be gained from the fact that each lorry carried around 50 churns of milk, which was then cooled at the depot before being loaded onto rail tankers for despatch to London.

In the same year that the Lostwithiel contract started — and more than a decade after the idea had been put forward as a means of tackling competition from road hauliers — the Great Western finally introduced a 'Collection & Delivery' service linking farms with GWR stations and dairy facilities, using its own road/rail tankers. These began operating in February 1932, and further investment from the company saw it establish concentration or collection points at such locations as Bridport and Yeovil. The new venture came rather too late to make a real impact on a business already dominated by others, but a few months later the *Great Western Railway Magazine* reported the introduction of a new type of railway wagon to carry the 2,000gal milk-tank road trailers that had recently been introduced by the GWR. Designed to 'expedite the transit of milk in bulk from the country to the big centres in the Company's system', the new wagons were vacuum-fitted to allow their use on express train services. The article noted that a valuable feature resulting was the ease and speed of loading and unloading at the beginning and end of the journey; the tractors that conveyed the road trailers simply towed the milk tanks onto the rail trucks using a wire pulley. When loaded on the rail truck the milk-tank trailer, which weighed 14 tons, was

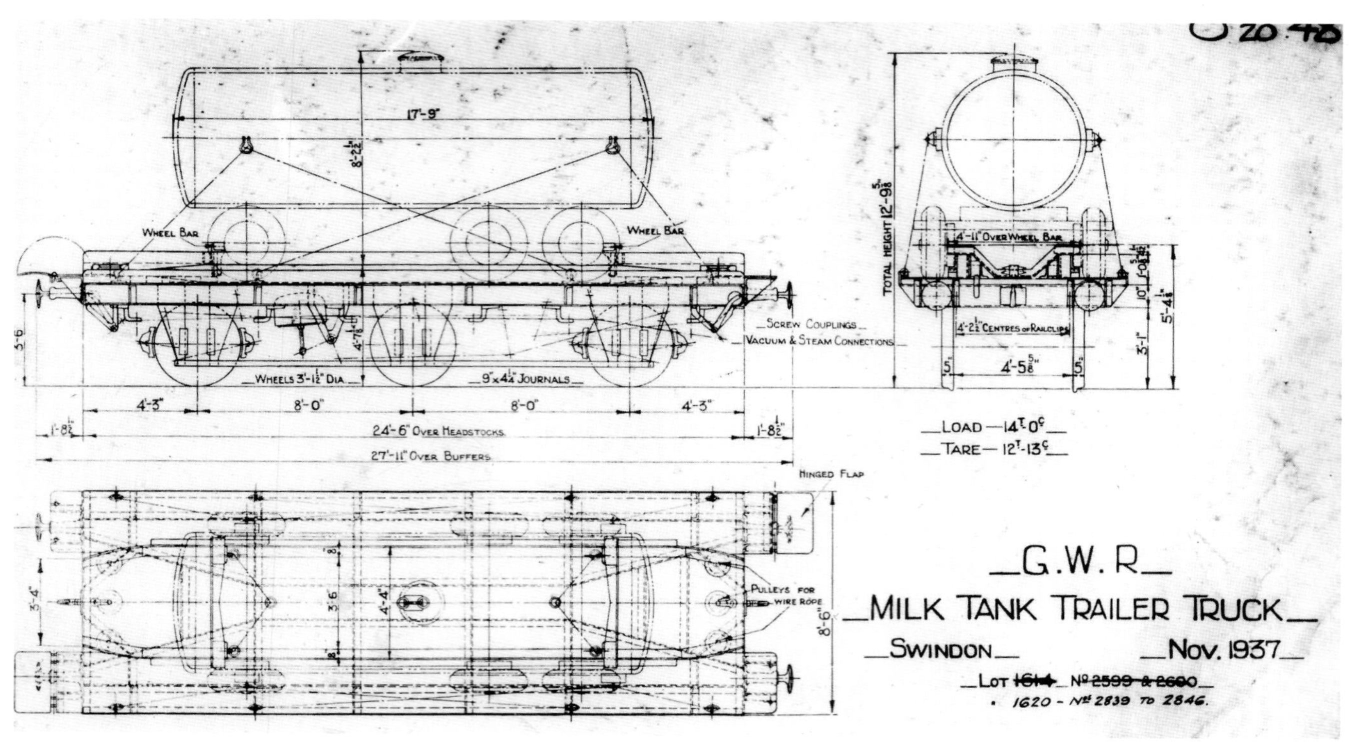

BELOW An official diagram for wagons built to carry road milk tankers, dated November 1937.

suspended by steel drums that removed weight from the tyres of the trailer during the rail journey. Wagons of this type were often marshalled into larger trains of the six-wheeled milk wagons, which eventually became commonplace on the railway.

Creameries operated by companies like Nestlé and United Dairies also provided much business for the GWR; such facilities, whilst often acting as collection plants for milk, produced and processed a wider range of products from the raw milk supplied in churns by farmers. Although many were situated close to main-line stations, in order that milk could be transported rapidly to urban areas, some were to be found at more remote locations. One of the best known on the GWR network was the depot and creamery at Hemyock in Devon, at the terminus of the Culm Valley branch, a short line with a main-line connection at Tiverton Junction, on the Bristol–Exeter route. Passenger traffic on the branch, opened in 1876, was always modest, and the dairy represented a major source of income, at least six (and sometimes as many as a dozen) 3,000gal milk-tank wagons being despatched every day. As traffic was light, many trains were mixed; empty milk tanks were delivered with the first train of the day, which arrived at Hemyock at 7am, and the 5.55pm service ran in the opposite direction from the terminus with full milk-tanker wagons. The branch was one of those already noted that had no passenger service on Sundays, but a locomotive was nevertheless required on that day to haul empties to the dairy from the junction in the morning and collect loaded tanks in the afternoon for forwarding to London.

ABOVE The Milk Concentration Depot built by the Nestlé company at Lostwithiel in 1932. A variety of GWR delivery lorries stand ready in the yard.

Considerable changes were made to the terminus at Hemyock when it was rebuilt in 1929, and a new spur siding was laid into the dairy. The processing plant had been built in 1886 by the Culm Valley Dairy Co, and, unlike that at Lostwithiel, it had its own fleet of more than a dozen lorries to collect milk from local farmers. Although it provided supplies of pasteurised milk for London it also produced butter, cheese and condensed milk — and, in later years, dried milk, ice-cream powder and cream.

3000 GALLON GLASS LINED MILK TANK
6 WHEELED – TWIN TANKS.
LOT. 1548
DIA. O.41
NOS. 2547 TO 2558

NEG C.O.C. 37.
PHOTO'D 27 SEP. 1935

ABOVE **The dairy and creamery at Hemyock were served by trains running on the Culm Valley branch. Pictured at the terminus is a train comprising three milk tanks and a single carriage, the latter more than sufficient to accommodate the modest number of passengers using the line.**

FACING PAGE TOP **A stainless-steel road milk tanker securely strapped to its wagon on 27 May 1932.**

FACING PAGE BOTTOM **A more unusual six-wheeled wagon featuring twin milk tanks, built for the London Co-operative Society in 1935.**

As well as empty milk tanks, branch good trains also delivered coal for the creamery's boilers and empty tins for dried milk. Locomotives were not permitted to run on the dairy siding, so empty milk tanks were left at the gate and drawn into the factory by winch; loaded tanks were returned by gravity, station porters being alerted of their approach by dairy staff who would bang the wagon buffers with a large spanner!

It would appear that, despite their best efforts in ensuring the rapid transport of milk from farmyard to dairy and on to the consumer, not all of the GWR's staff were fully alert to the perishable nature of processed dairy products. In 1929 the company's management was moved to issue two circulars, the first, in August, reminding staff that, following complaints about delays in the transport of cream, they should take great care 'to ensure that the traffic is kept out of the sun as far as possible' and that, on arrival at its destination, it should be taken to the Parcels Office and placed in 'a cool position to await delivery'. In December the same year, 'following a strong complaint', a further reminder was required, warning staff not to load butter too close to heating apparatus. Clearly there was still a problem some years later, staff being reminded once again about the transport of cream, this time in cans from the Wilts United Dairies plant at Melksham; complaints had been received from the dairy company, and care was to be taken 'especially when loading into and out of trains and on platform barrows', the circular concluded.

M N O P Q R
1 2 3 4 5 6 7

UNITED DAIRIES

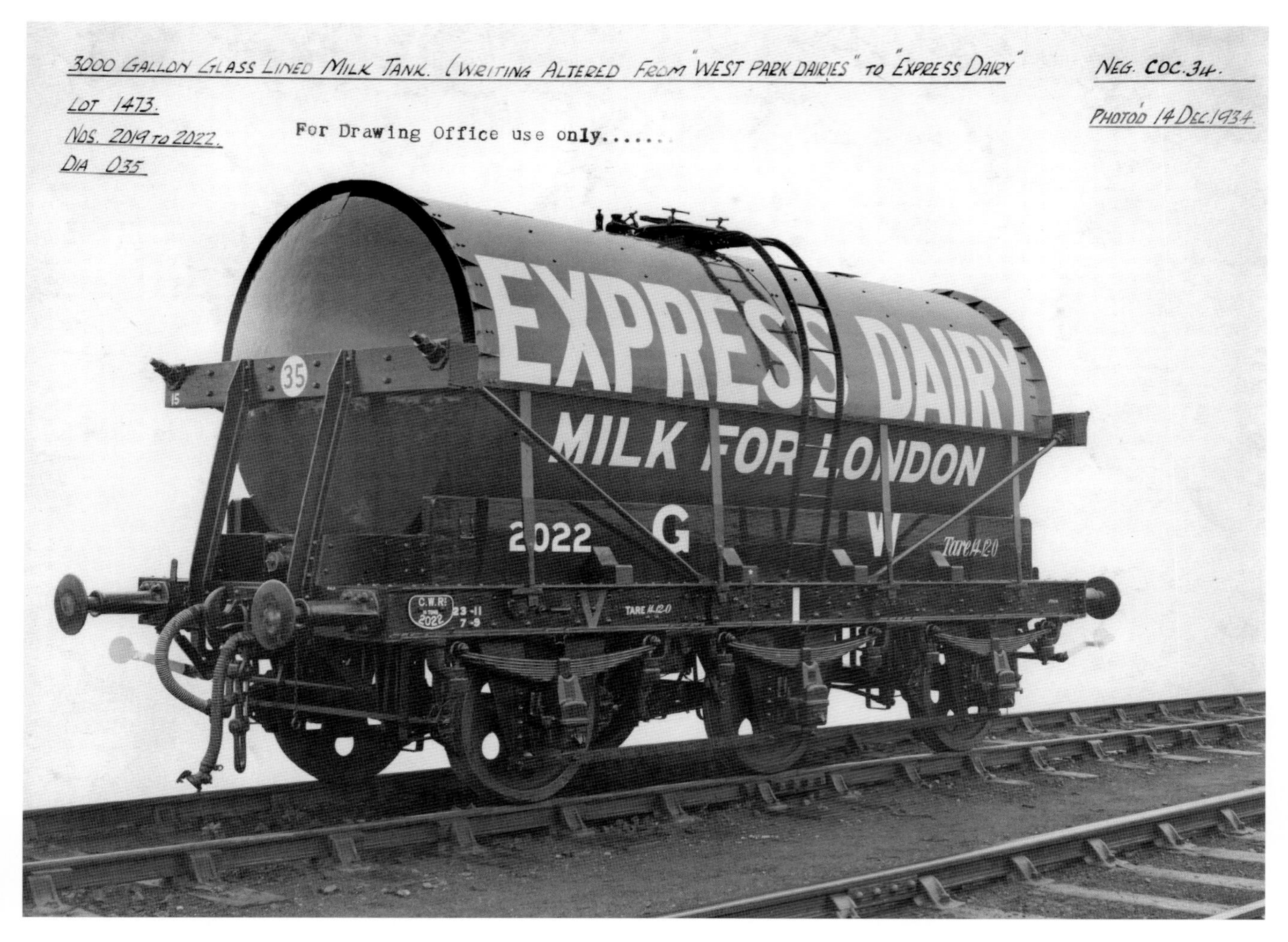

TOP LEFT The exterior of the modern facility at Wood Lane, operated by United Dairies on land leased from the GWR. It opened in 1935.

BOTTOM LEFT Milk is pumped from rail tanker wagons at the Wood Lane processing depot in London. As can be seen from the photograph, the plant could handle both milk-tanker traffic and the traditional churns, which remained in use until well after World War 2.

ABOVE A print from the drawing office at Swindon Works showing alterations to a 3,000gal milk tank in 1934.

PART 3: SUMMER

Although for both the public and railway staff the beginning of British Summer Time marked the approach of warmer weather and the impending holiday period this change was normally effected some weeks ahead of the traditional summer months of June, July and August. Moving the clock forward by one hour and the corresponding change back in the autumn nevertheless provided the railway with some logistical problems, as emphasised by a handbill issued by the General Manager's Office at Paddington in 1925. In that year Summer Time began at 2am on Sunday 19 April, and the handbill noted that there were 17 main-line express trains that were *en route* at 2am, among them long-distance services such as the 9.15pm from Paddington to Cardiff, Swansea, Carmarthen and Neyland, the 12.30am Paddington–Penzance and the 11.50pm Bristol–Crewe; these, along with branch-line trains and nine connecting trains running after 2am, were to run one hour later than the time shown in the company's timetables, the handbill recorded.

Before the much-anticipated rush of summer-holiday and excursion business on the Great Western, staff had another seasonal traffic to deal with. The start of the summer season

ABOVE **Bishopsteignton, between Newton Abbot and Teignmouth, was the setting for a number of pictures of the 'Cornish Riviera Limited' taken by the company photographer. This view features streamlined 'King' 4-6-0 No 6014 *King Henry VII* not long after modification in 1935.**

LEFT **A charming photograph showing the kind of temporary office used by the GWR at agricultural shows all over its network. Such offices not only co-ordinated the movement of livestock to and from shows but also, as the selection of posters illustrates, promoted the company's own passenger services.**

signalled the beginning of a series of agricultural shows and fairs that were staged in towns and villages all over the network and which generated considerable work and income for the railway. The work undertaken included carrying livestock of all types and running excursions and special trains that carried visitors to the shows. Some idea of the scale of the business can be seen in a report submitted by the Bristol Superintendent in 1930. In that year there were 17 agricultural shows held in the division; the smallest, held in August, was the relatively modest Beaufort farmers' event, which involved the movement of only five wagons into and six out of Badminton, the nearest GWR station to the show. Larger events included the Frome Cheese Show and the Bath Horse Show, each of which required the movement of more than 50 vehicles. By far the largest show held in the area was the Bath & West of England. Held annually at a number of different locations until finding a permanent home at Shepton Mallet in the 1960s, the show was extremely popular with both the rural community and people from larger towns and cities like Bristol, Bath and Taunton. The Bristol Diaries frequently note 'very heavy traffic' to the event and also record the number of special trains operated to move livestock in and out of the show. Smart work by staff was required to move cattle, sheep and other animals off the site quickly after the close of the event, trains being despatched at regular intervals through the night, and it was not uncommon for the railway to handle and load more than 200 wagons in a 12-hour period. As well as livestock, the Great Western also provided a collection and delivery service for agricultural equipment and produce displayed or sold at shows. In the case of the Bath & West event the GWR charged 4s each for 'hay rakes or other bulky articles', while for produce like butter, cheese, honey and other items contained 'in parcels not exceeding 28lb' the charge was 6d per parcel.

The large numbers of people attending shows provided the railway with a great opportunity to run excursion trains and offer specially priced tickets to generate further trade. This approach was not confined to larger events like the Bath & West of England show but was also employed for smaller events or fairs, like the Somerset Agricultural Show. When this particular event was held at Weston-super-Mare in May 1925 the GWR conveyed only 200 passengers on the first day, 1,500 on the second and a further 600 passengers on the final day. In the case of the Wiltshire Agricultural Show, held a month later at Warminster, the company advertised cheap return tickets to the town 'from any station

ABOVE New rolling stock was introduced on the 'Cornish Riviera Limited' express in 1929. This official view, recorded on 3 July by the Swindon Works photographer, shows the carriages being taken on a trial run to Stoke Gifford.

RIGHT A mocked-up photograph, produced in the 1930s by the GWR's publicity department, purporting to show keen holidaymakers on their way to the West Country. Sporting equipment, including a set of golf clubs and a couple of tennis racquets, is much in evidence.

within a radius of 60 miles, at the ordinary single fare plus fractions of a penny for the return journey'. A surviving internal staff notice gives details of livestock trains run following the end of the same show and provides a real insight into rural life in the 1920s, listing both the destinations and type of livestock moved. Only two special trains were required, the first, at 5.30pm, consisting of just two horseboxes and eight cattle wagons. The two horses were bound for Hungerford and Sparkford respectively, the first horsebox being detached at Trowbridge to be taken on to its Berkshire destination by a later train, and the second detached at Westbury for its onward journey to Somerset. Other wagons in the same train were bound variously for Bathampton, Woodborough and Radstock. The second 'special' left Warminster at 9.30pm and was rather longer, consisting of 28 wagons (including nine horseboxes), and carried pigs and sheep as well as cattle. The most distant destinations for the livestock wagons were Reading and Marlow; the Reading wagon contained two horses and the Marlow only a single cow, which could hardly have been cost-effective for the railway. Another wagon, containing 10 sheep, was bound for Sutton Scotney, in Hampshire, on the old Didcot Newbury & Southampton railway route, and two other horseboxes were sent back to Foss Cross station, on the old Midland & South Western Junction line to Cheltenham. In addition to the two special trains, seven wagons containing cattle, sheep and pigs were moved from Warminster on the same day as part of ordinary timetabled trains.

Whilst the loading and despatch of livestock from agricultural shows was normally accomplished without too much difficulty this was not always the case, and a memorandum issued by the District Goods Inspector at Swindon on the 25 August 1925 after the Marlborough Sheep Fair & Sale a few days earlier reveals that all did not always go to plan. Three of the scheduled special trains due to leave the Wiltshire town had departed more than three hours late as a result of a number of difficulties, among them the late arrival of wagons from Swindon, but the delay was due principally to the inadequacy of goods facilities at Marlborough High Level and Low Level stations. The showground was located more than a mile from both stations, meaning that drovers had little choice but to drive their flocks of sheep from the fair along local roads and then stay with them in the station yard or outside the goods yard while they waited for wagons to become available. Loading continued well after dark on account of the delays, and the chaotic situation was made worse by fact that there were no lights in the station yards, which must have made the job of herding and loading tired and irritable livestock something of a trial for station staff.

Matters were rather more straightforward at Kington in 1938, according to a *Great Western Railway Magazine* article published in September. The annual sheep fair at the Herefordshire town provided the company with 'one of its busiest livestock days of the year', more than 22,000 sheep being available for sale that year. Special exits were provided from the sale yard to the nearby station, where 200 wagons were kept in readiness; the loading of wagons was 'a brisk business', and the first of a number of special trains comprising 30 wagons left the goods yard at 2pm, to be followed two hours later by one of twice that length. A final consignment 'a quarter of a mile long' departed at 6pm, concluding a very busy day for GWR staff at the station.

In the years between the two world wars the fortunes of the GWR's goods business in respect of agricultural shows, sales and such events were on occasion severely affected by outbreaks of foot-and-mouth disease. In the 1920s in particular this was a real problem, and in the years 1922-4 there were more than 4,000 recorded incidents, leading to the slaughter of thousands of cattle, sheep and pigs. Although matters improved somewhat in the 1930s, in 1937 it was reported that the area served by the GWR's Bristol Division was once again seriously affected, and a number of fairs were cancelled as a result of the embargo on the movement of livestock, shows at Chippenham, Trowbridge and Melksham being particularly affected. Despite these difficulties the traffic handled at cattle and sheep fairs and larger agricultural shows continued to make a substantial contribution to the company's receipts in the interwar period and continued to do so until the use of road transport became more widespread. In 1930 it was reported that, in the Bristol Division alone, almost £4,000 of income had been earned from the movement of show and fair livestock, without accounting for the additional passenger and excursion traffic generated as a consequence.

ABOVE A farmer keeps a watchful eye on livestock waiting to be loaded at a country station in the 1930s.

In an article in the *Great Western Railway Magazine* in 1924 the company boasted that its arrangements for handling strawberry traffic warranted 'a little well-justified self-congratulation'. The strawberry season could be divided into two distinct phases, it added — the 'home and the foreign'. Mention has already been made of the handling of strawberries and other early fruit and vegetables imported in the springtime from the Continent through the Great Western ports at Plymouth and Weymouth and their distribution to the capital and other towns and cities, and his operation was followed in early summer by what the railway called 'strawberry time in the countryside', when domestic crops of this table fruit were harvested and brought to GWR stations for loading and distribution. While strawberries were produced in farms and smallholdings all over the GWR network, those grown on the southern slopes of the Mendip Hills were renowned for their quality, and the Cheddar Valley in Somerset could boast the greatest concentration of growers on the GWR network.

ABOVE **One of series of photographs taken by the company on 21 August 1926. In this view featuring the 'Torbay Limited' the guard has his back to the camera and passengers seem in no hurry to board the train.**

TOP RIGHT **One of the busiest locations on the GWR network on summer Saturdays was Newton Abbot. The station forecourt appears relatively quiet in this photograph, which also reveals that the station café was 'Open on Sundays'.**

BOTTOM RIGHT **A postcard view recorded at Cheddar and featuring GWR staff loading strawberries into wagons for despatch to London and the rest of the network. As the picture shows, wagons were fitted with shelves allowing baskets of fruit to be secured for the journey.**

The Cheddar branch, opened in 1869, generated very little traffic apart from 'tourists and strawberries', according to one writer, and indeed was nicknamed the 'Strawberry Line', even though the handling of this traffic was concentrated in three or four weeks of very intense activity, both at Cheddar itself and at a number of nearby stations, notably Axbridge, Draycott, Lodge Hill, Sandford & Banwell and Winscombe. Such was the scale and importance of the traffic that instructions were sent out to staff well in advance of the beginning of the season. 'Every effort will be made to meet the requirements of the traffic and ensure expeditious transit thereof,' wrote General Manager Felix Pole in a memorandum issued to staff on 22 May 1922, the document detailing the various destinations of trains from the Cheddar Valley, which included not only the Midlands and the North of England but also Scotland and Ireland.

During the brief strawberry season 'no one works harder than the station staff', a *Great Western Railway Magazine* article noted in 1924, and such were the demands that at the height of the season additional porters were drafted into Cheddar from other stations in the division. From dawn to dusk, each of the 300 or so growers in the area delivered fruit to the station, sometimes returning with further loads. Although fruit was loaded into wagons that could be attached to scheduled branch-line trains it was noted that the 'great event of the day' was the despatch of the 'Strawberry Special', which might comprise more than 10 'Fruit D' ventilated wagons, each 'loaded shelf to shelf to their utmost capacity'. In most cases growers had identified markets for their fruit and labelled consignments with their destinations, larger towns and cities being allocated specific wagons. The distinctive smell of strawberry permeated the train 'from engine driver to guard' and was 'guaranteed to make the most stolid traveller dream wistfully of sunny country gardens,' the article concluded.

RESTAURANT
CAFE OPEN ON SUNDAYS
REAT WESTERN RAILWAY
PARTIES CATERED FOR

ABOVE This atmospheric view of Worcester, recorded in May 1945, is full of detail but also shows spare carriage stock stored in sidings pending use in the summer.

Although foot-and-mouth and other diseases had devastating consequences for livestock farmers it was the British weather that caused most anxiety to strawberry growers. Warm and dry weather in spring and early summer, welcomed by holidaymakers and tourists, was not good news for farmers or the GWR; writing to the Superintendent of the Line in August 1922, the Divisional Superintendent at Bristol reported that strawberry traffic on the Cheddar Valley line was down by more than 60 tons due to 'light crops caused by exceptionally dry weather' during May and early June, resulting in a drop in revenue of £487 from the previous year's figure. Similar conditions were reported in 1930, when a larger decrease in income — £638 over the previous year — was noted, due to 'rain coming too late to save the crop'.

Goods services, including trains run to transport summer crops of strawberries but more especially those carrying goods to and from the industrial areas of the Midlands and South Wales, consistently earned more revenue for the GWR than did its passenger business, and by 1936 goods receipts accounted for 58% of income, a figure that increased when revenue from the company's dock operations was included. Although its passenger services were 'more in public prominence, it is the mineral and merchandise trains which earn a very large part of the revenue of the railways,' wrote W. G. Chapman in one of the company's books for 'Boys of All Ages' in 1923. Whatever the reality, the perception of the general public and passengers on the railway supported the GWR's claim that it was 'The Holiday Line' — a title it had maintained and promoted since the early part of the 20th century. 'While assisting in the development of industry in every district served by the company,' boasted a 1925 publicity booklet, the GWR was 'in a position to cater for holiday-makers, no matter what form of recreation they desire ... Wild mountain scenery, breezy uplands, moorlands, restful seaside resorts or fashionable watering-places' were all to be found within the confines of its network. Its routes provided passengers with connections to North and Mid Wales, the Welsh borders, 'Shakespeare Country' and what it called 'the more picturesque parts of the West Midlands', as well as the Wye Valley, Gloucestershire and the Thames Valley. Most importantly it served the beautiful counties of Wiltshire, Dorset and, particularly, Somerset, Devon and Cornwall, where much of its activity was concentrated in the summer months.

The holiday resorts, historic towns and cities and picturesque countryside served by the GWR, while providing it with a good source of income from passenger services, also presented it with a particular problem that was perhaps less significant to the other four 'Big Four' companies. Although it operated a full timetable of express passenger trains between all the major towns and cities on its network, along with cross-country and branch-line services, its high dependence on the holiday and tourist trade meant that by far the largest percentage of GWR passenger traffic was concentrated in the summer months, in particular at weekends. The contrast between summer and winter could scarcely have been more pronounced; David Wragg records that in 1938 and 1939 to run the summer service required an additional 800 trains on weekdays and a further 600 on Sundays; as he observes, how the railway could cope with such pressure for around 10 weekends in the summer period and remain profitable is difficult to imagine. David St John Thomas, meanwhile, noted that 'Nowhere else in Britain, perhaps the world, was the traffic pattern so enormously different,' concluding that it was 'yet another of those Great Western peculiarities'.

The seasonal fluctuations presented the GWR with two specific challenges, the first having enough locomotives and carriages to cope with the increase in demand, the second being able to cope with the additional numbers of passengers whilst avoiding excessive delays and congestion. In the case of the former there was, not surprisingly, much attention and planning to ensure that locomotives sent to Swindon Works for overhaul in the winter months were available by the summer. In addition, following his appointment as General Manager in 1921 Felix Pole made significant alterations to the way in which the railway operated, changing old and cumbersome working practices that had existed in the Locomotive Department, which supplied the motive power and footplate staff, and the Superintendent of the Line's Department, responsible for the timetabling and running of services. In 1923 the board agreed arrangements for 'co-ordination of train and engine working', which meant that the two departments were now jointly responsible for the allocation and distribution of motive power, the preparation of locomotive working diagrams, the timing and alteration of train services and the hours worked by enginemen. There was also a move to place 'as much responsibility as possible ... in the hands of local officers', inspectors hereafter reporting to local divisions rather than to Swindon. All this meant that at busy periods, particularly in the summer months, there was far more co-ordination between departments, enabling delays to trains to be kept to a minimum.

Providing enough carriages to cope with summer demand was a further issue. The Great Western was forced to build and retain additional coaches which for much of the year were stored out of use in large carriage sheds around the network and at the headquarters of the Locomotive, Carriage & Wagon Department at Swindon. Work was, of course, required to check, clean and prepare stock each spring, unless it had been used in the interim for other specials or excursions such as those run for football matches or other sporting events outside the summer season. In the 1920s and 1930s the Great Western invested further in carriage sheds and sidings; addressing the GWR Lecture & Debating Society in Bristol in 1930, Mr R. G. Pole, the Divisional Superintendent there, outlined some of the work being undertaken to improve Bristol Temple Meads using investment from the Government's Development (Loan Guarantees and Grants) Act 1929. In the course of his lecture Pole gave an interesting insight into the facilities and numbers of carriages required to operate services all year round. He noted that the approximate number of coaches and vans in regular daily working that were stabled at Bristol ranged from 300 during the winter to 330 in the summer but that extra room had to be found for

ABOVE RIGHT **Churchward '47xx' 2-8-0s were normally used on express freight trains, but on busy summer Saturdays they were often pressed into service to haul passenger reliefs, as was the case here with No 4707, seen passing through Dawlish.**

RIGHT **A 1930s view of a Prairie tank bringing a portion of the up 'Cornish Riviera Limited' out of St Ives.**

ABOVE The scene at Bristol Temple Meads on 31 August 1923. Heavy bank-holiday traffic meant that the Penzance–Wolverhampton train seen leaving the station was double-headed.

another 100 or so coaches that included stock for excursion trains and special saloons, resulting in a total of more than 400 carriages for Bristol Division alone. One of the last schemes to be implemented under the terms of the 1929 Act provided the GWR with further covered storage capacity and consisted of a large carriage shed built close to Swindon Works; more than 1,800ft long, this could accommodate 265 coaches and was completed a few months before the outbreak of World War 2 in 1939.

The GWR's board and management were all too aware of the problems caused by the surge of demand for its passenger trains in the summer months, and, writing in the company magazine in June 1927, Felix Pole reminded staff of efforts made in an 'Earlier Holidays' campaign that had sought to encourage people to avoid the summer months when booking their holidays, reiterating that the advantages of earlier holidays were 'longer days, cheaper hotel accommodation and less overcrowding on trains and at resorts'. The promotion of this idea had begun in the years just after World War 1, when the Great Western was still struggling to bring its service back up to prewar standards, notwithstanding maintenance backlogs and coal shortages. In 1920 the number of trains being run was still 25% down on that for 1914, the company reporting at the time that the difficulties then faced by the railway would be 'materially minimised' if passengers could be induced to take their holidays in spring or autumn. There was also some evidence that earlier holidays might produce better weather for holidaymakers; in the 1930s an analysis of records at the Meteorological Office revealed that July, August and September had higher rainfall totals than did June, which month also boasted higher average sunshine totals in the quarter-century to 1933.

No matter how hard the Great Western tried in its advertising campaigns, the reality was that many people were unable or unwilling to take their holidays out of season; during the interwar period most people were restricted to taking their annual break during the school holidays in July and August, and (in comparison with the situation in more recent times) families had much less flexibility in terms of when they could begin their holidays, which resulted in huge peaks in traffic on summer Saturdays. Another factor was that many workers were not entitled to any paid holiday at all; in 1938 it was calculated that only 8 million of more than 18 million people earning up to £250 per annum were entitled to paid leave, and, for those that were, entitlement was normally limited to one week plus bank holidays.

This state of affairs naturally placed a great strain on GWR staff, stations and trains in the summer months; reporting on a number of very busy weekends in 1925, including the August bank holiday, the *Great Western Railway Magazine* noted that traffic had been 'exceptionally heavy' and had necessitated the running of the 'Cornish Riviera Limited' in no fewer than three separate sections on Saturday 2 August, on which day practically all the other major expresses were run in two portions. In addition the GWR ran numerous excursions and carried many other holidaymakers from the capital on what it termed 'ordinary trains'. The congestion was not confined to Paddington, however, the company reporting that traffic from the Birmingham area was also 'exceedingly heavy', extra trains being required for destinations on the Cambrian Coast and the West Country.

To cope with the increased demand the company usually operated a special summer timetable, an exception being 1926, when a shortage of locomotive coal — a consequence of the General Strike some months earlier — necessitated a continuation of winter timings. The precise details of the summer timetable varied from year to year, depending on anticipated demand and

BELOW Staff from the Great Western's publicity office in Bristol stand outside 4 High Street. The office looks rather neglected and indeed was about to make way for an extension of a local department store. On display in the window can be seen two GWR jigsaws, along with a copy of *Holiday Haunts*.

the success or otherwise of the previous year's arrangements. In 1934 a *Great Western Railway Magazine* article outlined the special features of that year's timetable; the train services planned had, it noted, been reviewed in the light of the experience gained from the introduction in 1933 of 'Summer' tickets on Saturdays, which had necessitated 'the duplication and triplication' of a large number of trains all over the system; as a result additional trains had been timetabled 'to obtain a more suitable distribution of passenger carryings'.

A brief description of some of the changes made in 1934 clearly illustrates the way in which the company reacted to the surge in demand in the summer months. On Saturdays, to relieve pressure on the 10.30am 'Cornish Riviera Limited', a new West of England express departed Paddington at 9.30am, running non-stop to Plymouth before calling at the principal Cornish stations; another West of England express, calling at the same places, was timetabled to leave the capital half an hour after the 'Cornish Riviera'. In a further attempt to ease congestion on Saturdays the GWR provided a new sleeper service, which left Paddington at 11pm on Friday, running non-stop as far as Plymouth and finally reaching Penzance at 7am on Saturday.

To cope with increased demand from returning holidaymakers and trippers the timetable was bolstered during the summer months by additional trains in the up direction. In 1934 these included a new 9am Saturday express from Perranporth, which called at St Agnes, Truro and Liskeard, thereafter running non-stop to Brent, over the county border in Devon, where it picked up passengers from the Kingsbridge branch, before continuing non-stop to Paddington, arriving there at 3.45pm. Further evidence of increased passenger numbers on summer Saturdays was the fact that the weekday 11.10am Penzance–Paddington, which called at Newton Abbot, Exeter, Taunton and Westbury, was replaced by no fewer than four new advertised trains from the West Country to London. Each stopped at a different combination of stations, the first, from Penzance, drawing passengers from mostly Cornish locations, the second, which began its journey at Dartmouth, calling at Teignmouth, Dawlish, Exeter, Taunton and Westbury; a third service left Paignton at 2.45pm, calling at Newton Abbot and Torquay before running non-stop to Paddington, while the final train departed Newquay at 12.30pm, stopping only at Par and Plymouth on its journey to the capital.

Additional trains were also provided on cross-country routes; two new trains connected Paddington and Cheltenham, whilst a further innovation was the introduction of the 9.10am Wolverhampton–Weymouth Sunday train which called at principal stations and ran via Oxford, Swindon and Westbury, reaching the Dorset resort at 2.32pm, a return train departing just over two hours later. Extra trains were also introduced to run between the West of England and the Midlands, running via Bristol, as was a special Saturday-only express from the West

ABOVE A GWR express leaves the holiday resort of Weston-super-Mare. To the right are the four platforms of Weston-Super-Mare Locking Road station (originally opened in 1866 as 'Weston-super-Mare Excursion Platform') and where carriage stock is stabled waiting returning excursionists later in the day.

Midlands to Weston-super-Mare; the Bristol Channel resort was always a favourite destination for holidaymakers from Birmingham and the Black Country, and this train left Smethwick Junction at 9.35am, reaching Weston at 1.44pm. Further services ran from Birmingham via the North Warwickshire line. Welsh destinations too were served by a variety of new trains, an added innovation being that the new Birmingham–Cardiff services were worked by the GWR's recently introduced diesel railcars. Some sense of the scale and scope of its annual summer timetable can be gleaned from the fact that the company was able to announce that it had introduced more than 900 new train services in July 1934. In more difficult economic conditions, however, it could not always maintain this level of service, and by the outbreak of World War 2 five years later the total had dropped by around 100.

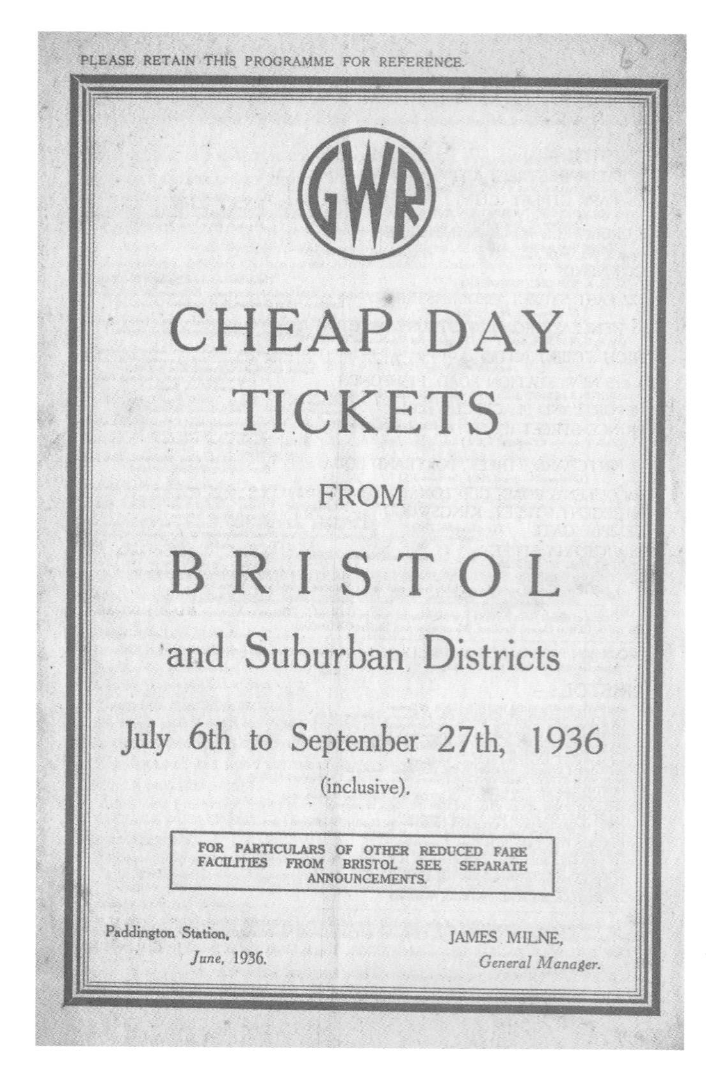
PLEASE RETAIN THIS PROGRAMME FOR REFERENCE.

GWR

CHEAP DAY TICKETS

FROM

BRISTOL

and Suburban Districts

July 6th to September 27th, 1936

(inclusive).

FOR PARTICULARS OF OTHER REDUCED FARE FACILITIES FROM BRISTOL SEE SEPARATE ANNOUNCEMENTS.

Paddington Station,
June, 1936.

JAMES MILNE,
General Manager.

LEFT GWR booklet detailing excursions from the Bristol area in the summer of 1936.

TOP RIGHT A 1927 view of a Paddington–Weston-super-Mare express hauled by 'Castle' 4-6-0 No 4098 *Kidwelly Castle*.

BOTTOM RIGHT The growth in excursion traffic to the new resort of Severn Beach, near Bristol, meant that more-substantial passenger facilities were required than the simple platform provided initially. The station buildings shown here were completed in 1923, a year after services began.

Although income from passenger traffic declined from almost £14 million in 1925 to just over £11 million in 1937, as a result of both the Great Depression and the increasing effects of road competition, the Great Western continued to experience huge peaks in its passenger traffic during the summer months. At major stations such as Paddington, Birmingham Snow Hill and Bristol Temple Meads and also at smaller intermediate and junction stations all available staff were on duty to cope with long days of intensive traffic. Taking their own holidays during such periods was not easy; the minutes of a Divisional Managers' meeting held in Bristol in March 1922 record that 'all present were impressed with the desirability of arranging for the junior members of the staff to take their holidays in the spring previous to the heavy summer traffic'. While this measure may have helped ensure that staffing levels were somewhere near the level required to cope with increased traffic, on occasions the company was forced to employ temporary staff or even to bring porters back from retirement on peak summer weekends.

The hustle and bustle of Great Western summer traffic has been described by a number of railway writers; David St John Thomas noted that a 'special atmosphere of anticipation pervaded West Country stations' on summer Friday evenings as staff contemplated the busy days ahead. This anticipation was felt all down the line and most especially at resorts served by the Great Western as the proprietors of guest houses and cafés, hoteliers, taxi drivers and even deck-chair attendants hoped for good weather and large crowds. In its *Speed to the West* booklet, published in 1939, the company boasted: 'There must be few people who do not know, at least by hearsay, that the West Country is ideal for summer holidays; the cliffs of Cornwall, the sands of Devon, the hills of Somerset and the mountains of Wales — all of these have long been famous as summer holiday playgrounds'. Many stations in Devon and Cornwall handled almost 90% of their long-distance passengers in the course of a few days each year, and on summer Saturdays a constant stream of trains deposited holidaymakers from Paddington, South Wales and the Midlands; while developments such as new cut-off lines constructed in the 1930s improved matters, beyond the Royal Albert Bridge at Saltash trains to Cornish destinations completed the final leg of their journey rather more slowly than they had started it.

The Cornish main line was very busy with through services running to seaside locations such as Newquay, Perranporth and St Ives. Although traffic to the Royal Duchy had been growing in the years before the Great War, in the interwar period Cornwall became increasingly popular as a holiday destination, as more middle-class families could afford to take a break in July or August. During this period the St Ives branch was normally worked with a two twin-coach 'B-set' formation, supplemented by a further Third-class carriage on Thursdays and Saturdays in summer, when more than 100 extra passengers were expected. In addition both the 'Cornish Riviera Limited' and any relief trains following it included three carriages for St Ives. By 1938 demand had increased further, so that often four or even five extra carriages were required on these services. Extra trains were also run on the busiest day of the year, August Bank Holiday; Stanley Jenkins in his portrait of the line noted that on those days the branch train had a locomotive at either end to avoid the need to

BRITISH RAILWAYS
PARCELS OFFICE
& CLOAK ROOM

ABOVE **Holidaymakers throng the beach at Barry Island, although, judging by the dress of many of those shown on this postcard, the weather was not particularly warm.**

run round at the seaside terminus when trains were packed with day-trippers and holidaymakers.

Staff at stations like St Ives sometimes struggled with the large amounts of luggage sent by holidaymakers in advance or brought with them on trains, as evidenced in August 1929, when a plea was issued by the Divisional Superintendent at Plymouth asking staff to make a 'thorough search' for a two-wheeled sack trolley which had been missing since 17 July; this was branded 'St Ives' and had clearly vanished in the holiday rush. The huge quantities of luggage transported by the railway also prompted the GWR to publish a booklet on the subject in May 1934; 'What a pleasure it is to meet on your journey the carefree traveller,' it exclaimed, 'one who looks not on personal luggage as just an unfortunate necessity ... but a very material component in the development of complete holiday enjoyment.' The 12-page booklet provided passengers with instructions on how to label their luggage, information on the cost of transporting bicycles and perambulators and details of the 'luggage in advance' system, which, the company claimed, for 'quite a nominal charge luggage is collected, conveyed and delivered to the destination address'. Spared taxi or cab fares, transfer charges and porterage, the traveller was thus 'free from luggage worries or baggage anxieties, and travels unhampered to participate fully in the joy of the journey'.

When the weather was fine the number of holidaymakers and trippers using the GWR network could be enormous, particularly on the August Bank Holiday weekend; the Bristol Diaries kept by the Divisional Superintendents Office at Temple Meads station include a number of reports by staff and press cuttings taken from local newspapers describing Bank Holiday traffic. In an article titled 'Record Rush by Bristol Holidaymakers', published just before the 1935 August Bank Holiday, the *Bristol Evening Post* reported that trippers were 'escaping business cares' and that 'trains were running in triplicate'. It would be the biggest holiday rush in years, it continued, arguing that 'it's going to be warm and dry', as the weather experts were in agreement this time. They were indeed, and the bank-holiday weekend proved to be hot, with brilliant sunshine, although the large number of trains calling at Temple Meads would have left the station's hard-pressed staff little time to appreciate it. More than 100,000 passengers passed through the station, among them 35,000 bound for Weston-super-Mare and 13,000 for Weymouth, described by the newspaper as 'the Naples of England'.

In 1937 another record-breaking bank holiday was recorded, a headline in the *Bristol Evening World* proclaiming 'Hot News: It is the best day of the year'; the ensuing article described crowds sleeping on the beach overnight at Weston-super-Mare and men 'shaving in public toilets'. The sunny weather experienced by holidaymakers that year meant that Weston enjoyed by far the biggest day in the resort's bank-holiday history, the *Western Daily Press* reporting on 3 August that well over 100,000 people (a 'sea of humanity') had been crammed into the Somerset resort; of this total more than 37,000 had come by train, arriving at either the main Great Western station or the excursion-train platforms at nearby Locking Road. Impressive those these numbers were, for the railway a more worrying statistic must have been that 35,000 people were reported as having arrived by car. Elsewhere on the railway similarly high passenger numbers were recorded; those for long-distance passengers were 'certainly the best we have had for a number of years', according to a Great Western official quoted in the *Bristol Evening News*. The hot weather also brought the railway a problem of a different seasonal nature. In the weekly instructions issued just before the bank holiday in 1938 staff were advised that 'Messrs J. Lyons & Co anticipate despatching large quantities of Ice Cream traffic from Kensington (Addison Road) during the August Bank Holiday week-end' and warned that, because of warm weather, 'the best arrangements should be made to ensure expeditious transits and deliveries'; if ice cream were to arrive at a station after the delivery van had left for the day, the consignee was to be telephoned immediately to arrange collection. Staff were also asked to ensure that during the summer all empty ice-cream containers were returned to Lyons, especially during the August bank-holiday weekend.

Owing to the fickle nature of British weather, not all August bank holidays were quite as busy as those described above; on 7 August 1922 the Divisional Superintendent at Bristol wrote to Paddington, reporting 'very heavy day-trip traffic, notwithstanding the fact that it rained heavily all day yesterday and was cloudy and somewhat threatening this morning until up to mid-day'. It was noted that approximately 18,500 passengers were conveyed in trains to Weston-super-Mare and around 5,000 to Weymouth and Portland. The poor weather meant that resorts closer to Bristol were busy, traffic to Portishead, Clevedon and Burnham amounting

ABOVE The beach at Weymouth, seen at the height of the holiday season in August 1929.

to more than 6,500 passengers. The Divisional Superintendent was also able to record that 7,500 passengers had been carried to a new resort on the banks of the River Severn near Pilning, around 15 miles from Bristol. Severn Beach was established on what had been a farm, until the GWR constructed a new line linking Avonmouth and Pilning, opened in February 1900. The route was not actually used for passenger traffic for well over 20 years, until 1922, when a new excursion platform was completed to serve the new resort. The first trains to use Severn Beach Platform were special excursions from stations in the Bristol area run over the Whitsun bank-holiday weekend, a regular timetable of trains being operated from July until the August bank holiday, when an excursion-only service was once again provided. A handbill issued to promote the first excursions noted that the new platform was situated 'amid delightful sylvan surroundings' and that a 'sand and shingle beach extends for over one mile and a half along the banks of the Severn', adding that bathing was 'practicable' at all states of the tide.

The modestly sized platform provided initially at Severn Beach meant that the total of 7,500 passengers carried over the 1922 August bank-holiday weekend was probably the highest then practicable; the following year, however, the GWR built a more substantial permanent station that enabled it to cope with much greater numbers, the new facilities including an additional platform provided specifically for excursion trains. In 1924 an all-year-round train service from Bristol was inaugurated, and the riverside resort began to grow, acquiring all the requisite facilities expected by visitors, including shops, amusements, a boating lake and a large hotel, the most popular attraction being the 'Blue Lagoon' swimming pool, built in 1933. The more fanciful dubbed the resort 'the Blackpool of the West', but many Bristolians were rather less charitable, dubbing it 'Severn Beach on the Mud'.

BELOW The view from the platform ends at Aberystwyth, featuring the locomotive shed and yard, as recorded by the company in 1937.

ABOVE **The GWR steamship *St Julien* arrives at St Helier in June 1925.**

Whatever its reputation, Severn Beach remained a very popular destination, both among the residents of Bristol and with excursionists from farther afield; over the August bank-holiday weekend in 1935 the railway conveyed more than 13,000 passengers to the resort, which continued to be busy during the summer until well after World War 2.

Severn Beach was among the destinations listed in an extensive programme of period and weekend excursions produced by the GWR for the Central Wales Division over the 1929 August bank-holiday weekend, although it was possible to reach the South Wales resort of Barry Island. Period excursions were the equivalent of what would now be called off-peak return tickets, available at 1⅓ times the cost of a single ordinary ticket, and were valid on any train on Tuesday or Wednesday, return being permitted on any train the following Tuesday or Wednesday; for shorter trips weekend tickets were issued at the same rate. The Central Wales Division encompassed stations in North Wales, such as Whitchurch, Ellesmere and Wrexham, and much of the old Cambrian network in Mid Wales and around Cardigan Bay. The 24-page booklet advertised excursions that covered much of the GWR network, and passengers travelling to London from Mid Wales for the bank holiday could do so via a number of different routes; a seven-hour journey awaited passengers from Builth Wells, whose route took them via Talyllyn and Newport, while those departing Rhayader at 10.17am would not reach Paddington until after 5pm, the train travelling via Welshpool, Shrewsbury and Bicester. Other long-distance trains run on Friday 2 August took holidaymakers to resorts in Devon and Cornwall, notably Torquay, Falmouth and Penzance, the advertised return trains running a week later.

For those wanting a shorter break the Great Western ran a number of special trains from the industrial and coal-mining towns of North Wales to Aberystwyth, the most important holiday destination on the Cambrian Coast. One service called at intermediate stations such as Welshpool, Montgomery, Newtown, Caersws and Moat Lane, while another took in stations on the line from Brecon, including Talgarth and Builth Wells. On Saturday 3 August an excursion ran in the opposite direction on the latter route, enabling holidaymakers to travel to South Wales, changing at Brecon for stations to Cardiff and beyond. There were also numerous trains to resorts in North Wales, such as Rhyl, Colwyn Bay and Llandudno, as well as services to the Midlands and the North of England. Among the more expensive trips offered by the GWR was one to the Isle of Man via Birkenhead, from where passengers took a ferry to Liverpool, there to board the steamer to Douglas. The fare from Aberystwyth was 29s 6d Third class, with 'steerage' accommodation on the steamer, and 37s Third class with 'saloon' accommodation on the steamer, the journey to the Isle of Man taking around eight hours.

Resorts like Weston-super-Mare and Weymouth attracted large numbers of holidaymakers and excursionists not only over long distances but also from adjoining counties like Gloucestershire and Wilshire. GWR excursion trains ran via quite circuitous routes, in order to pick up as many passengers as possible. In his history of the Malmesbury branch Mike Fenton notes that no fewer than 10 seaside excursions to Barry Island, Paignton, Weston-super-Mare and Weymouth were run in August 1936; to reach Barry Island, passengers from Malmesbury had to travel via Patchway, there to join an excursion originating from the Somerset town of Frome. The roundabout routes traversed by these trains meant that many trippers returned at a late hour, a Malmesbury-branch train running from the junction at Little Somerford for the benefit of returning excursionists.

ABOVE The port of Looe was a popular destination for holidaymakers, being served by a branch from the main line at Liskeard.

ABOVE An attractive colour illustration of the GWR's premier express, as reproduced on the back of a 1920s booklet promoting winter holidays.

Fenton also describes special excursions run by combined Sunday schools in the area; in June 1936 one 10-coach train for Weston left Malmesbury at 8.50am, returning with its load of tired children and their equally tired parents just before 9pm. The historic Wilshire town also benefited from GWR excursion traffic itself, although clearly not on the scale experienced by seaside resorts. In the 1930s the railway ran popular day excursions from Paddington to Westbury on the third Sunday of every month, enabling passengers to visit a variety of historic sites in Wiltshire. At around noon a branch train was despatched from Malmesbury to Wootton Bassett to collect visitors to the town, returning later in the day to connect with the excursion train as it made its way back to the capital; this operation necessitated special arrangements, for apart from the morning milk train no timetabled services ran on the branch on Sundays.

Mention has already been made of the large numbers of trains run to the Dorset port of Weymouth. In June 1925 excursions from Cardiff, Newport and Paddington were run to what the company called 'the healthy, sunny and beautiful Wessex coast'; on Sunday 21st four trains from South Wales and three from London deposited almost 5,000 passengers at Weymouth. These trains provide good indication of the level of business generated from summer-holiday traffic to the resort; an advertisement in *Holiday Haunts* boasted that Weymouth, 'The charming resort in Hardy's Wessex', was a place of 'record sunshine, golden sands, sea and sun bathing'; visitors could also take advantage of facilities for golf, tennis, bowls, yachting and fishing and see a 'super revue production with orchestra' at the town's Alexandra Gardens Theatre. Although many travelled to Weymouth to take in the 'Health, Sunshine and Pleasure' offered by the resort, a goodly number passed through *en route* to the Channel Islands, embarking on one of the company's steamships. During the winter months the level of patronage — and the sometimes stormy weather conditions in the English Channel — meant that services to Jersey and Guernsey operated only on alternate days, but in the summer the GWR was able to offer sailings every day except Sundays.

A regular steamer service between Weymouth and the Channel Islands had operated since 1794, although it was not until 1889 that the GWR began its own ferry service. Following a period of intense competition with its rival, the LSWR, which also provided a steamer service to the islands, an agreement between the companies in 1899 enabled new joint arrangements to be introduced whereby the GWR provided daylight services only, the LSWR operating overnight services with return daytime sailings. Following the Great War and the Grouping the joint arrangement continued with the new Southern Railway, although it soon became apparent that the facilities and ships provided by the GWR for the Channel Islands service were in need of updating.

Matters were substantially improved in 1925 when, in addition to the construction of two new cargo ships placed in service to handle the conveyance of fresh flowers and produce described in Part 1of this book, the Great Western took the opportunity to introduce two new passengers ships. The *St Julien* and *St Helier* were modern turbine steamers capable of accommodating up to 1,000 passengers, each with facilities far superior to those on the ships they replaced. 'The comfort of the passengers has been carefully studied,' claimed company publicity at the time of their introduction; sleeping berths were now confined to the lower decks rather than being located in dining saloons and public areas, as they had been on earlier ships, and cabins were provided with running water. Given the sometimes dangerous nature of the waters around the Channel Islands, the ship's hull was divided into 12 watertight compartments to give greater buoyancy in the event of a mishap.

Even after the introduction of the two new ships the GWR was sometimes hard pressed to cope with the volume of business in the busy summer season. It was reported at the end of 1925 that 'passenger traffic to the Islands had been a record during the summer' and that 116,647 passengers had been carried, an increase of more than 30,000 over the previous year. This figure was doubtless boosted by extending the period of daylight operation by five weeks, from the end of June until the end of September, but, noted a company report, the new steamers were considered to be 'of great advertising value'. June 1925 had also seen the introduction of a special boat-train service, leaving Paddington at 9.30am and calling at Reading, Bristol and Westbury before reaching Weymouth at 12.37pm. The steamer departed Weymouth just over an hour later, at 1.55pm, reaching Guernsey at 5.25pm and Jersey two hours later.

To cope with peaks in demand the GWR provided as a standby an additional ship, the *Great Western*, normally used on the Fishguard service. This vessel provided extra capacity each Saturday in August — an arrangement that endured until 1930, when it was replaced by a new ship, the *St Patrick*, which was a replacement for earlier vessel of the same name that had sunk after catching fire the previous year on the Fishguard route. The new *St Patrick* thus fulfilled a dual role, being regularly employed on the Fishguard–Rosslare service but also as a relief boat for the Weymouth–Channel Islands route. It could carry 1,000 passengers, although there was sleeping accommodation for only 216 in First class and 116 in Third. The level of comfort provided again represented a distinct improvement over earlier vessels used on cross-Channel services, and the location of bars, saloons and other catering facilities was 'specially planned to meet the maximum demand which occurs in the summer season,' according to the *Great Western Railway Magazine*. It was also reported that the number of passengers conveyed by the GWR on both the Fishguard and Channel Islands routes had grown steadily from 1923 and that 1929 had been a record year, prompting the writer to anticipate that, with the introduction of a further 'splendidly equipped' ship, matters would improve still further. Reporting on developments in 1930, the Bristol Divisional Superintendent noted that having the capacity to operate an additional boat from Weymouth during the summer season 'continued to be appreciated and to attract additional passengers'. Demand for berths was so great on Saturday 2 August that a third relief boat was necessary, a total of 2,766 passengers travelling to Guernsey and Jersey, and 946 making the return journey; in all some 30,106 passengers were carried between 12 July and 20 September 1930 — an increase of nearly 6,000 over the same period the previous year.

The *St Patrick* nearly came to grief two years later, on 5 August 1932, when it hit rocks off the coast of Jersey. The ship had 295 passengers and 49 crew aboard and had left Weymouth at 1.40pm in fine weather, but as it approached the island thick fog restricted visibility, and the vessel hit rocks off La Corbière, flooding the engine room. With watertight doors closed there was no danger of the *St Patrick* sinking immediately, and passengers were subsequently transferred to a Southern Railway ferry, the *Isle of Sark*. The GWR ship was eventually towed to Plymouth for repairs costing over £6,000, and a subsequent Board of Trade report ruled that the wreck had been 'caused by the wrongful acts and default of the master', Captain Charles Waine Sanderson. Given his previous good record, the master was fined £100 and censured, and the railway could count itself fortunate that there had not been more serious consequences arising from the incident, especially as three ships had been lost in similar circumstances in the past.

In addition to the scheduled services GWR ships were used to operate day cruises and excursions to the Channel Islands and other locations, such as the Isles of Scilly and Cherbourg. Often these trips were part of a longer itinerary that included a train journey from locations on the Great Western network; in 1930 16 'Marine Excursions' were recorded in the Divisional Superintendent's annual report, with passengers drawn from Birmingham, Bristol, Cardiff, Exeter and Reading. For the five excursions run to Cherbourg the 987 passengers were given a 'road motor tour' as part of the package, earning the company the princely sum of £17 in commission.

The GWR provided road motor tours on home soil too, and a booklet advertising 'Day and Half-Day Trips' from the Cambrian Coast resort of Aberystwyth for the summer months of 1929 lists more than 20 different tours provided for holidaymakers, most

ABOVE **The sands of Carbis Bay are occupied by only a few holidaymakers as a two-coach train makes its way along the St Ives branch towards the Cornish terminus in the 1930s.**

concentrated in the area around Barmouth and Towyn and in the heart of Snowdonia. Some trips were run with GWR vehicles, such as a daily trip around Talyllyn Lake, at the foot of Cader Idris, while others used local coach companies. The No 4 Circular tour, which encompassed a rail journey to Portmadoc and then a 'Grand Motor Ride of 50 Miles' through the Pass of Aberglaslyn and Llanberis, used coaches supplied by J. Williams & Sons. The same train to Portmadoc also enabled Great Western excursionists to travel to the summit of Snowdon, a coach ride to Llanberis being followed by a trip on the mountain railway to the top of Wales' highest peak.

Back in the West Country, the throng of holidaymakers and tourists visiting Weymouth in the summer months was swelled by an annual invasion known to the locals as 'Swindon Week'. The resort was one of the favourite destinations for Great Western staff and their families taking advantage of the 'Trip' holiday arrangements provided each year by the company and the Mechanics' Institution. Introduced in 1849 as a day excursion to Oxford for employees of the railway works and their families, 'Trip' grew as the works expanded, ultimately becoming a whole week when the factory shut down and staff could take advantage of a free ticket to a destination of their choice. Beginning on the first Friday in July and continuing until the following Monday week, it presented the opportunity for a break from the noise, grime and tedium of the works, although because the holiday was unpaid until 1938, when the Holidays with Pay Act was passed, many Swindon families could not always afford to stay away all week. Even after the introduction of paid holiday, workers usually received only half the wages they would have expected, as holiday pay was paid at a flat rate and not calculated using the piecework rates that applied during the rest of the year.

In the years before the Great War more than 25,000 people left Swindon during the 'Trip' holiday period. Although 'Trip' ran as

LEFT Swindon staff and their families pose happily for the camera at Swindon Junction station in 1932 as they wait to board trains to the West Country and a host of other locations. Most 'Trip' trains departed from sidings in the works rather than from the station.

BELOW LEFT A contrasting scene in the carriage works at Swindon, as Trippers pose for the camera in rather more cramped circumstances on 8 July 1932.

usual in July 1914, the following year it was announced that on account of the war it would not take place, although there was still some hope that it might be possible to reschedule the holiday to September or early October. Such optimism turned out to be misplaced, and 'Trip' holiday did not actually resume until July 1919. Some 22,000 people, no doubt worn out by four years of conflict, took advantage of the first postwar 'Trip', more than 5,000 visiting Weymouth and 7,000 travelling to the West of England. As the country — and the railway and Swindon Works in particular — slowly recovered from the war, the number of Trippers steadily increased, such that in 1924 it was recorded that more than 29,000 workers and their families went on 'Trip'. Most travelled on what was traditionally known as 'Trip Friday'; in that year the railway ran 31 special trains consisting of a total of 520 coaches in an intensive eight-hour period, beginning with a number of overnight services to the West of England and other, more distant locations.

The movement of so many people in a such a short period of time naturally put a great strain on the railway's operating staff; surviving handbills and instructions give some idea of the preparations required — not just at Swindon, for the departure of trains, but also at some of the larger resorts, where holidaymakers would arrive in great numbers. Staff were drafted in from elsewhere on the network, and a 1922 instruction noted that additional guards and ticket collectors from locations such as Bath, Chippenham, Gloucester, Stapleton Road (Bristol) and Westbury had worked at Swindon on the first day of that year's 'Trip'. The same instructions also requested that stationmasters at Weston-super-Mare and Weymouth in particular should ensure that guards and station staff had taken their rest days before the day Trippers were due to return to Swindon at the end of their holiday; such was the pressure at Weston that in 1922 an additional nine platform staff were booked to cope with the rush.

The pressure on the railway in the busy summer period led to an appeal by management to Swindon staff to stagger their departure dates in order to avoid the traditional crush of 'Trip Friday'. Chief Mechanical Engineer C. B. Collett told staff in 1925 that the previous summer 'very great difficulty was experienced by the company in dealing with passenger traffic, particularly during the week-ends', and they were 'earnestly requested' to see if they could begin and end their holidays during the middle of the week. Collett concluded by arguing that this request was being made to facilitate the working of traffic and hoped that there would be 'hearty co-operation' to prevent a repetition of the difficult working problems experienced the previous year. As Rosa Matheson noted in her history of 'Trip', this idea was not popular with landladies and hotel owners, who normally booked their accommodation from Saturday to Saturday. In 1930 the company went further, moving the beginning of the holiday to Monday — a tactic which did not work, as almost 30% of the staff did not take up their free 'Trip' ticket and instead booked Privilege tickets to travel on the weekend anyway; the number of tickets booked meant that the railway had to provide four extra trains, defeating the object of the exercise.

Matters having returned to normal, the *Great Western Railway Magazine* reported in 1933 that the town of Swindon 'was depleted of half of its population in a few hours on the night of

13 July, when GWR staff and their families left for their annual holiday'. The exodus that year involved 31 trains and the movement of 27,416 people; more than 23,000 of this total left on 24 trains in a period of less than four hours, a staggering statistic rightly described by the magazine as 'a piece of organisation without equal in the world of transport'. It was also reported that Trippers travelled to no fewer than 350 different resorts, although the majority confined themselves to the destinations listed in the table (right).

As already noted, Weymouth was the most popular seaside destination, closely followed by Weston-super-Mare. Weston was often the choice of families who simply could not afford to be away for more than a day; the relatively short train journey meant that Trippers could arrive at 7am and not leave the resort until around 8pm. The less-well-off also took their own food, making them unpopular with shopkeepers and café owners, although oral-history testimony reveals that public houses did benefit, as workers deserted their families on the beach for a pint or two in a local hostelry. The Cornish town of St Ives also developed a special relationship with Swindon workers and their families, and despite a seven-hour journey by the late 1930s around 1,000 Swindonians were visiting the fishing village and resort; the large numbers sometimes caused problems, but in general there were friendly relations between locals and trippers. An annual event was a charity cricket match between locals and railway families, proceeds being donated to a Children's Outing Fund in Swindon; this generosity was reciprocated by an annual collection at the railway workshops in aid of the St Ives Lifeboat.

The sense of gloom naturally felt by Swindon railway staff and their families following their return from 'Trip' in late July lifted for one weekend a few weeks later, when the Great Western Mechanics' Institute Fête was held in Faringdon Road Park. Usually held on the second Saturday in August, the 'Children's Fête', as it was more normally known by local people, was eagerly anticipated each year. The park, close to the estate of houses built by the company for its workforce in the 1840s and opposite the railway church of St Mark's, had been provided by the Great Western but in 1929 was transferred to the ownership of the town council in exchange for land on which a new carriage workshop was built on the other side of the existing works. For the fête the park was transformed into a huge fairground, and for days in advance the streets around the railway village were full of wagons and lorries, the contents of which were unloaded the night before. For an admission ticket costing 3d children attending the fête could take advantage of the rides, swings and stalls that were ranged around the park; they were also entitled to a ½lb slab of fruit cake (made locally and sliced using a machine manufactured in the works), enjoy a ride on a roundabout or swing and have a cup of tea or oatmeal drink. The day was normally rounded off by a circus performance, such as a high-wire act, followed after dusk by a spectacular firework display.

Resort	Adults	Children
Weymouth	3,289	2,203
London	3,142	862
Weston-super-Mare	2,627	1,504
Barry	1,173	860
Teignmouth	562	294
St Ives	533	252
Blackpool	459	85
Newquay	426	107
Jersey	383	85
Tenby	311	121

The hot summer weather enjoyed by the children attending the fête in 1929 was, unlike the event itself, not annual occurrence. Peter Timms, in his account of life inside and outside the railway works during the 1930s, records a rather less enjoyable day in 1931 when heavy rain turned the park into a quagmire; the local newspaper reported that the bad weather meant that only a quarter of the 40,000 people who normally attended turned up, and that the traditional firework display was postponed until the Monday evening as a result.

The summer months could also be a time of severe thunderstorms resulting from prolonged spells of hot weather, severe flooding being the unfortunate result. The Bristol Diaries record that in both 1936 and 1937 the centre of the city was badly affected by thunderstorms and flooding, causing widespread damage. An article in the *Western Daily Press* for 16 July 1937, headed 'St Swithin Pays Bristol a Visit', reported that the storms had left a 'trail of damage, destruction and dampness' and that almost 4in of rain had fallen within 24 hours. The article went on to describe the effects of the deluge on unfortunate residents and businesses in various parts of the city, as well as disruption to transport links; many roads were flooded, and the GWR was also badly affected, Stapleton Road and Clifton Down stations bearing the brunt of the worst flooding. Company records note that at 9am the thunderstorms caused a culvert carrying a sewer under the railway at Lawrence Hill station to burst; the result was a flood of filthy water that reached 4ft above the level of the railway lines, requiring all traffic to be stopped. Two hours later the water had subsided, but no sooner had services recommenced than another cloudburst closed the line again, and all was not 'properly opened' until 6pm. When summer storms hit, the effects of flooding were often more pronounced, drains overflowing as a result of being blocked with leaves and vegetation; trees heavy with summer foliage could also be blown over in high winds, blocking railway lines.

TAKING REFRESHMENT

Whilst the Hotels, Refreshment Rooms & Restaurant Car Department was by no means the largest on the GWR, the services it provided were nevertheless *vital* to the travelling public. The department could offer a level of efficiency 'second to none in its efforts to meet the requirements of the public', the company argued, whether it applied to 'the modest sandwich and a refreshing cup of tea' or a most 'elaborate repast' served by 'efficient attendants, with the accompaniment of the choicest wines'. In 1934 its staff numbered 1,536, a figure that included seven managers, 57 clerical staff, 80 'Inspectors and Manageresses' and 1,392 weekly paid staff.

The catering and hotels team was spread across the entire GWR network, many staff running refreshment rooms or restaurants at stations, others working at company hotels, and a smaller group serving passengers in tea, buffet and restaurant cars on the company's principal daily express trains. Every effort was made to provide these services 'at moderate charges for all classes', something desired and appreciated by customers, a 1930 guide to the department noted. The annual publication described both the facilities and fare offered by the GWR, giving details of not only its grandest hotels but also more modest restaurant and refreshment facilities provided at stations and on trains and steamships.

The management and operation of hotels promoted by the GWR in the 1920s and 1930s was not entirely straightforward,

BELOW Recorded in March 1926, this fine panoramic view of Fishguard Harbour illustrates not only the extent of the GWR's facilities there but also how close the Fishguard Bay Hotel was to the station and dock.

as the railway did not own all of them. In its publicity the company usually concentrated on its four largest — the Great Western Royal Hotel at Paddington, the Fishguard Bay Hotel, the Manor House Hotel at Moretonhampstead and the Tregenna Castle Hotel near St Ives. In addition it had interests in smaller hotels in places like Bristol, Plymouth, Taunton, although in reality most 'station hotels' were not railway-owned. Between the wars the Great Western invested heavily in its hotels, purchasing the Manor House Hotel and refurbishing others to ensure that they were as up-to-date as possible.

'First and foremost' was the Great Western Royal Hotel, which by the 1930s had been an important part of the Paddington terminus for more than 80 years. Opened in 1854, it had been modernised on a number of occasions, but by the early 1930s it had become rather outdated and was in need of modernisation. By 1939, however, the company was able to report that it had been transformed into one of the most modern and comfortable hotels in London and that it had entered 'a new era'. The GWR board's decision in 1927 not to proceed with a radical and far-reaching redevelopment of Paddington (which would have involved the demolition of Brunel's original trainshed) had left the way clear for extensive work to be undertaken at the hotel in order to bring it up to modern standards. The completion of a new block saw a 'luxurious' foyer, lounge, smoking room and cocktail bar added on the ground floor; air-conditioning was provided, and the dining room updated, the work also including the provision of a new 'Grill Room' accessible from Praed Street.

Above the public facilities, which included a 'spacious lounge and cocktail bar', were four floors providing single and double bedrooms, some with sitting rooms. The refurbishment meant that bedrooms now had hot and cold running water *en suite*, 'the majority with private baths'. Double-glazing was also fitted to reduce noise from both London traffic and the almost continuous activity taking place in the station close by. An advertisement in the summer timetables for 1938 revealed that single rooms with a private bathroom cost 12s per day, a double room of the same type costing 18s; three-room suites were provided at a cost of 51s per day. Breakfast, lunch and dinner were extra, a further

ABOVE A later view of the Fishguard Bay Hotel. A sign on the gatepost on the left indicates the tradesmen's entrance, whilst the bridge connecting the hotel and gardens can clearly be seen at a high level.

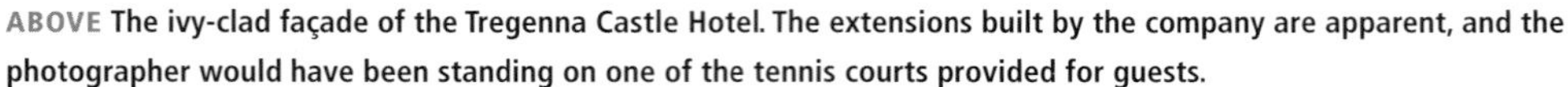

ABOVE The ivy-clad façade of the Tregenna Castle Hotel. The extensions built by the company are apparent, and the photographer would have been standing on one of the tennis courts provided for guests.

ABOVE A youthful GWR hotel porter, photographed in 1922.

additional charge being made if meals were served in private rooms. Servants were accommodated on the fifth floor, and the tariff supplied by the company showed that this accommodation cost 7s 6d per day, excluding meals. Refreshment Committee minutes record the considerable investment made at Paddington; in October 1936 £44,000 was allocated to the hotel, this being followed by a further £55,000 in July 1937. A year later more than £15,000 was made available to create a new banqueting hall.

An undated booklet issued by the GWR described facilities at the Fishguard Bay Hotel, many miles from Paddington, in West Wales. Previously known as the Hotel Wyncliffe, it had been taken over by the company in 1906, when Fishguard 'made its debut in the world of travel'. This being the port of arrival and departure for the GWR steamships operating the route to Ireland via Rosslare, the necessity for a good hotel was readily apparent, and the company wasted no time in 'supplying the want', the hotel being conveniently situated close to the quay where passengers embarked.

GWR publicity made much of the hotel's unique position, arguing that besides affording shelter from the winds that would no doubt have blown in from the Irish Sea it had views of 'great extent and rare beauty'. The company booklet describing 'luxuriant pine woods' that provided a picturesque backdrop, and to design the landscaped gardens surrounding the hotel the Great Western employed the services of a Cornish florist, who took 'every advantage of the affinity between this part of the western coast of Pembrokeshire and the Cornish Riviera'.

The hotel had 40 bedrooms and provided accommodation for 50 visitors, several complete suites of apartments being available. There is little doubt that it had enjoyed its best years before the Great War when the West Wales port was at its busiest; after 1918 it was less successful. The minutes of the Hotels & Refreshment Rooms committee meeting held October 1937 recorded the approval of new expenditure of £2,500 to install lavatories in 34 bedrooms at Fishguard, along with an additional nine bathrooms and a cocktail bar. Such efforts to modernise the facilities must surely have been motivated by a desire to generate more business, for by the mid-1930s, a time when all the other GWR hotels were prospering, the Fishguard Bay Hotel was reportedly making 'small losses'. Guests were warned that cheques would not being accepted as payment, and 'visitors arriving without luggage and not being personally known' were required to leave a deposit. An extra charge was also due if meals were 'not partaken of in the hotel'.

In typical GWR fashion company publicity boasted of the 'phenomenal mildness' of the climate at Fishguard, suggesting that it was not only a place to stay when travelling to and from Ireland but also a destination in its own right. In addition to 'sub-tropical gardens of great extent and beauty' the facilities

ABOVE A motor omnibus was provided to ferry guests from the GWR station at St ives to the Tregenna Castle Hotel. This bus, based on a Burford chassis, was used from 1922 to 1929, when it was replaced by a new Thornycroft.

LEFT A 1920s poster produced by the GWR to promote its Tregenna Castle Hotel at St Ives. The tennis courts shown in an earlier photograph are in use, while the hotel's golf course is also featured among the amenities.

provided for guests included a billiard room, library, croquet lawn and hard tennis court. A nine-hole golf course was also available nearby at Cwmbrandy; 'charmingly situated on the southern slopes of the bay overlooking the magnificent harbour and Irish Channel, the course adds to the natural attractions of this ideal health and pleasure resort at all seasons of the year,' the hotel guide informed guests. There were also two pages dedicated to fishing; as elsewhere, the company had acquired fishing rights for its guests, in this case on the nearby River Cleddau. The river was suitable for trout fishing, although the riverbank was 'rather soft' in places, guests were warned. Whilst fly-fishing was allowed 'worm fishing' was not permissible, and any fish less than 8in long were to be returned to the river.

The Tregenna Castle Hotel was located at the heart of the Cornish Riviera — 'England's unequalled Holiday land', according the GWR's Hotels Department. Described as a 'holidaymakers' resort set in the wonderful country of The Lizard and Kynance Cove, of Tintagel, of Sennen and Land's End, where gaunt cliffs frown down on the swirling waters of the Atlantic', it was said to combine the 'old-world charm of the higher-class English mansion with modern improvements which tend to make hotel life comfortable and attractive'. Opened in August 1878, the hotel and its extensive estate had been owned by the GWR only since 1895; previously leased, the imposing square-turreted granite mansion had been built some 150 years earlier on a wooded hill close to the fishing town of St Ives, with its steep, narrow streets and bustling harbour, its origins being reflected in the company's publicity, which portrayed it as 'the perfect example of the hotel which is no hotel', enjoying the atmosphere of a comfortable country house. It could accommodate more than a hundred guests and stood in its own park and gardens, unspoiled and apparently unmodernised. Appearances were, however, deceptive, and the addition of new wings in keeping with the original building provided more bedrooms, 'a number of which are provided with hot and cold water,' according to a company booklet issued in 1930; further improvements included a new lounge and dining room and the 'unobtrusive introduction of a well sprung dancing floor'. Other modern amenities introduced included central heating, telephones, electric lighting and white-tiled bathrooms. Clearly aimed at a well-heeled clientèle, the hotel, the hotel was described by the company as having the 'all-pervading atmosphere of comfort ... well-organised servants, perfect cooking and a wine cellar that has no equal outside London,' prospective guests being reminded that 'simplicity need by no manner of means be synonymous with an absence of the more material delights of the connoisseur'.

By 1938 the Tregenna Castle Hotel had been extended even further, to accommodate up to 160 guests, and bedrooms, many of which were now equipped with central heating, were provided with their own private bathrooms. The dance floor had also been extended, and, perhaps with a more elderly guest in mind, a new lift to the bedrooms had been installed. In a bid to encourage guests to remain in the environs of the hotel a nine-hole 'approach and putting golf course' had been recently built, the 'combination of the terrain and the ingenuity of the contractor in providing artificial obstacles' having produced a course which would prove 'a real test of skill for the keen golfer', publicity noted. The hotel also had six tennis courts, and in 1930 the GWR announced that it had provided a squash court, an 'entirely new and almost unique feature' for country hotels, devoted to the visitor 'desiring a more vigorous form of exercise'.

Much was, of course, made of the hotel's location, for surrounding it were more than 100 acres of park and woodland, which stretched almost as far as the beach at Porthminster and the 'indescribably beautiful' St Ives Bay. The gardens, featuring semi-tropical flowers and shrubs, were charming all year round, but a number of company publications argued that the best time to visit was spring, when 'the fields are yellow with buttercups and the deep silent woods fragrant with primroses and violets, or a misty haze with bluebells'; this was the time, noted the hotel guide, when 'wise men leave a bleak and chilly London and seek and find the wonder of Cornish woods and the recuperative value of ocean air'. The estate also had its own 'Home Farm', a well-run operation that provided the hotel with most of 'the delectable food served in its spacious and sunny dining room'. Fruit, vegetables, eggs, chickens and ducks could be supplied fresh to table from the gardens and farm, and a pedigree herd of Guernsey cows supplied the milk used to produce butter and thick Cornish cream, which was a feature of many hotel meals. The Tregenna Castle farm cattle won a number of awards at local agricultural shows; the GWR Hotel Committee minutes for July 1935 recorded that they had been inspected by the vet and that all animals were in a healthy condition and free from tuberculosis, 'with the exception of two' that would be re-tested shortly.

A further innovation in the 1930s was the provision of additional garages for guests and accommodation for valets and chauffeurs. The rise of the motor car for touring could not be ignored, and the same work was undertaken at the fourth of the

ABOVE A couple enjoy a round of golf in the grounds of the Manor House Hotel. The stream running alongside the course was clearly a hazard for the less-accomplished golfer, as a net has been provided by the hotel to allow errant golf balls to be retrieved from the water!

LEFT An impressive view of the Cornish fishing village of St Ives, recorded from the grounds of the Tregenna Castle Hotel.

GWR hotels popular between the two wars, the Manor House Hotel at Moretonhampstead, in Devon. Here 15 garages, with six rooms for chauffeurs and residential accommodation for garage attendants, was provided at another country-house-style venue. The Manor House had been acquired and converted by the GWR as recently as 1929, having previously been the home of Lord Hambledon and was situated in 200 acres of grounds. The company's directors discussed the possible purchase of what was originally called the Bovey Manor House in February 1929, the General Manager recommending that if it could be obtained for £15,000 the property should be purchased as soon as possible. Less than a month later, following an inspection by directors, it was reported that the Manor House had been acquired for £14,500, which sum included the billiard table, electric light fittings, curtains and carpets.

In the Hotels Department's annual report for 1929, reproduced in the company magazine for January 1930, it was noted that the opening of the new venue had been the highlight of the year and that work required before opening had included the installation of boilers, new kitchens and additional 'lavatory accommodation', at a cost of nearly £10,000. Constructed in the Jacobean style, the manor itself dated back only to 1907 but was an impressive building nonetheless; the oak-panelled interiors and 'tastefully' furnished large rooms produced a 'magnificent setting', Great Western publicity maintained, although pictures of the interior show a rather gloomy and old-fashioned look to the hotel. The annual report also noted that a new 18-hole golf course in the grounds of the hotel was also 'well on the way to completion' and would be one of 'the most sporting and enjoyable links in the West of England'.

The GWR's investment clearly paid off, for the company was able to report that following its opening on 15 August 1929 the Manor House Hotel had been full to capacity during the holiday period and that visitors had been 'loud in their appreciation of its appointment and of its magnificent situation'. However, its somewhat old-fashioned interior and facilities meant that that less than six years after its opening the hotel was modernised once again, central heating, electric lighting and a lift all being installed. The accommodation was increased, a new wing being

ABOVE The art-deco refreshment rooms and snack bar at Exeter St Davids, as photographed for the company in the late 1930s.

LEFT A 48-page booklet published by the GWR in 1947, by which time car ownership had begun to make significant inroads into the company's business.

added, and more leisure facilities were provided, including squash and badminton courts. Like the Fishguard Bay Hotel the Manor House was an attractive destination for visitors interested in angling, holding fly-fishing rights on the rivers Bovey, Bowden and Teign; some measure of the importance of fishing as a draw for guests can be ascertained from the fact that the GWR employed a river-keeper to watch the hotel's own waters — surely one of the most unusual jobs on the railway.

Whilst the four large hotels described above represented the most important part of its business the Hotels & Refreshment Room Department did consider a number of other schemes. The most significant proposal was for another hotel in Cornwall, at Looe. Minutes of the committee meeting held in July 1936 record that the cost of the proposed hotel and golf course was £187,000 and that the hotel would have been about the same size as the Tregenna Castle; the cost had, however, risen from previous estimates, it was left to the main GWR board at Paddington to discuss the matter in due course. If there were misgivings over the project they were not made explicit at the meeting, and the following year the acceptance of a tender for diverting the road between Millendraeth Beach and Seaton, at a cost of £5,214, was discussed. Two years later a further report was submitted on tenders received for the new hotel, but a handwritten note attached to the minutes reads 'Alternative scheme to be prepared'. The hotel plans had been linked with an ambitious scheme to build a new line to Looe via St Germans, which would have allowed a diesel-railcar service to be run from Plymouth to a new terminus in the resort, but by 1939 this project had been mothballed. Also discussed at some length during the 1930s was the proposed construction of a new hotel at Birmingham Snow Hill, but this project, estimated to cost £175,000, was not proceeded with before the outbreak of war in 1939.

Although the GWR did not proceed with a new hotel in Birmingham it maintained a significant presence in the city in the form of the station restaurant at Snow Hill, in what had been the old Great Western Hotel. This was highlighted by the company as typical of the refreshment facilities provided at larger stations; by the late 1920s the concept of the refreshment room was regarded as somewhat outdated, the company's stated aim being to 'take the fullest advantage of every modern development and service' in allowing the traveller to obtain 'just what he may require', be it a cup of tea from the platform, a light lunch box or tea basket to take on the train or a meal at one of the restaurants or dining rooms situated at larger stations. By the early 1930s tastes were changing, the GWR General Manager reporting to the board that in the company's cellars at its stations and hotels was a large quantity of vintage port and champagne for which demand was now 'negligible' and recommending that it should be sold at a reduced price. At the same meeting it emerged that there were more than 28,000 cigars that had been in stock for 'many years' and were not now in first-class condition; these too would be sold off cheaply. The restaurant at Birmingham was described as 'the luncheon rendezvous of the city', although it also served breakfast, lunch and afternoon tea. The Grill Room, access to which could be gained from Livery Street, was open from 8am until 10pm each day. The facilities provided for 'obtaining well-cooked and quickly served food at moderate prices are equal to any in the City of Birmingham,' a 1927 booklet boasted.

The rather grand facilities at Snow Hill were matched by the refreshment rooms to be found from 1923 on Platform 1 at Paddington. Located between the Royal Waiting Room and the General Manager's Office, these had been refurbished as a result of 'rapidly increasing business', the centrepiece being a large 'U'-shaped counter topped with marble sourced from a quarry on the GWR network, at Ashburton, Devon. They were decorated with 'fine marble columns and pilasters', the railway reported, this investment following the enlargement of the dining rooms elsewhere on the station, which was 'much appreciated in the summer season'. It was also noted that a new tea room was planned 'for those desiring the lighter form of refreshment'.

By the mid-1930s the GWR was providing rather more modern and informal facilities for its passengers at Paddington. The new 'Quick Lunch and Snack Bar' was opened on Platform 1 in 1935; distinguished by its art-deco bar in the shape of a horseshoe, it was capable of seating up to 38 people. At the centre of the bar

BELOW The grand interior of one of the company's refreshment rooms at Paddington, pictured in 1925

CHOCOLATES
TOBACCO
CIGARETTES
E. POLLARD & Co

HAIRDRESSING
PLATFORM No 1
REFRESHMENT
CONFECTION

TOP RIGHT The caption on the reverse of the original print claims that this tobacconist's stall was to be found at Paddington, although it seems more likely that the photograph was taken elsewhere on the GWR network. Partially visible on the left is a Nestlé chocolate-vending machine.

BOTTOM RIGHT The crowded platform at Oxford in 1930. On the right of the picture is one of the many confectionery outlets provided for passengers not wishing to patronise the GWR's refreshment rooms. *British Motor Industry Heritage Trust*

RIGHT For those not wishing to visit one of the refreshment rooms situated around Paddington station a number of trolleys were available on the platforms, offering passengers hot drinks and snacks for their journey. Crockery, usually marked with the name of the station, could be returned on a later train.

was a large showcase that also housed a hotplate, tea- and coffee-maker, waffle-maker and toaster. The art-deco styling was perpetuated throughout the room, which featured cream walls, and walnut, chromium and steel were used extensively in both the bar itself and other decor. Speedy and skilful service was provided by 'white-coated chefs', reported the *Great Western Railway Magazine*, and diners could choose from an extensive menu of hot and cold dishes that comprised hors d'oeuvres, soup, shellfish, poultry, salads, sandwiches and sweets, including waffles and gateaux; the range of sandwiches included various novelties, among them the 'Plymouth Hoe' (a meat sandwich) and the 'Paddington Three-Decker', which contained a variety of six different meats and fillings. The new bar also provided diners with 'Cornish pasties and other dishes which tell of the territory served by the GWR,' noted the company magazine.

Made possible by Government loans, the reconstruction in the interwar years of many of its stations also provided the GWR with the opportunity to modernise its refreshment facilities. In addition to those at Paddington, new restaurants and grills were introduced Bristol, Cardiff, Newport and Taunton, while further new facilities were provided at Weymouth and Plymouth, where a 'well-appointed' refreshment room was built to cater for the large numbers of passengers disembarking from ocean liners. The annual guide giving details of catering and refreshment facilities for 1936 even highlighted the 'vastly improved' dining and refreshment rooms now available at Swindon Junction; in the 1840s the station had been the location of the infamous refreshment rooms about which Isambard Kingdom Brunel had complained so bitterly. Swindon Junction was hardly the most salubrious location at which to dine while *en route*, but the suite of large banqueting rooms provided on the first floor of the station were used extensively by railway staff for meetings, dinners and dances.

An earlier survey of the GWR's catering facilities listed almost 100 on various lines all over the network, ranging from the larger refreshment rooms at locations such as Bristol, Cardiff and Paddington to the more modest provision at the likes of Dolgelly, Marlborough Low Level and Three Cocks Junction. At most larger stations light refreshments could be obtained, and in dining rooms hot and cold meals with a 'choice of wines' were available. 'Glasses of water are provided to travellers at all refreshment rooms free of charge,' the survey reported.

For passengers not wishing to take refreshment at station dining rooms or restaurants there were alternatives; 'wheel waiters' were large trolleys that were pushed up and down platforms at a number of 'stopping places' to enable passengers to 'obtain tea and a variety of light refreshments without leaving their seats,' the company reported, while at larger stations, for those interested in more healthy fare, there were also platform wagons 'devoted to a variety of choice and seasonable fruit'. It was also possible to obtain a GWR 'snack box' from one of the wheel waiters or a station refreshment room; known originally as a 'light lunch box', this contained sandwiches, cake and fruit and in 1936 cost 1s 3d. In the 1920s it was still possible for passengers to obtain baskets of food to take with them on the train. The 3s breakfast basket contained eggs and bacon, bread and butter, preserves and hot drinks, while lunch or dinner baskets, costing between 2s 6d and 3s each, included hot or cold meats (typically chicken and ham), cheese, salad and bread. Also available was a tea basket, containing a pot of tea or coffee, bread and butter, a cake or bun and fruit. All the baskets were equipped with the same GWR crockery and cutlery used in station refreshment rooms, which passengers left in the basket when the meal was complete. 'In view of the serious losses by breakage and otherwise of basket fittings, the Company ventures to solicit the co-operation of passengers to ensure their proper use,' it was noted in 1929.

For passengers travelling long distances perhaps the most comfortable and luxurious option was the restaurant car; introduced in 1896, this had rapidly become an essential component of the most important trains. In the years following the Great War

ABOVE **The interior of First/Third-class restaurant car No 9582, built by the GWR at Swindon in 1929. The rather gloomy decor harks back to an earlier (albeit refined) era on the railway.**

the company could boast that there were more than 70 restaurant cars 'in daily circulation throughout the main arteries of the Great Western system', notably between Paddington and the West Country, Birmingham, North and South Wales, Ireland via Fishguard, as well as on cross-country routes from the North of England and Scotland to Wales and the South West. It also boasted that its service was known for 'the well-cooked, good quality food and the excellent wines offered within the reach of all'. That said, the tariff for what it called 'ordinary trains' noted that luncheon cost 2s 6 or 3s and dinner 5s, which would have put eating on trains beyond the reach of many, given that at this time the average wage amounted to just £3 per week.

By the 1930s GWR restaurant cars were providing a more than 1.5 million meals a year. The whole operation of cooking and serving numerous sittings of breakfast lunch and dinner on a long-distance express service required excellent facilities, well-trained and skilful staff and the best-quality food. Aside from bread and rolls (specially delivered to Paddington six times daily by specialist bakers) and biscuits (supplied to the GWR by the Huntley & Palmer company in Reading) all ingredients used in restaurant-car meals were prepared on the train; as one writer commented, once it had departed there was 'no shop around the corner if anything is either forgotten or spoiled'.

On a typical journey from the capital a joint of meat would be prepared and placed in the oven of the dining car's kitchen long before departure time in order to ensure that it would be ready for serving *en route*; this would be done while the carriage stock was being cleaned and prepared at Old Oak Common depot before being taken back at Paddington to await its passengers. In the pantry and kitchen of the dining car staff carried out various tasks; salads were prepared, cheese sliced and soups and sweets completed ready for the stove. The 'kitchen boy', reported the *Great Western Railway Magazine* in 1938, was 'surrounded by cabbage and potatoes' and might have to peel up to a hundredweight (50kg) of the latter on a busy day; depending on the season and the menu, his job might also entail cutting up large quantities of French beans or gooseberries.

The kitchen, in which up to 180 meals could be produced, was tiny. Measuring just 9ft by 6ft, it nevertheless contained everything required; the six-ring gas stove took up almost half that space, and the rest of the equipment was crammed into every available space and cupboard under, above and around it. Hygiene and cleanliness being considered of paramount importance, the walls of the kitchen were lined with steel, and all other fittings and equipment chromium-plated. Pots and pans were the finest that British industry could produce, the company boasted, the capacity of a dining-car saucepan being 36 pints (21 litres). Care was required on the part of the chef and his staff to ensure not only to ensure that food was well prepared and on time but also that there were no accidents or injuries in the small kitchen as the train lurched and swayed. Once settled into the routine and surroundings, however, most chefs stayed with the company, enabling it to 'build up a staff of chefs second to none in the country,' noted the writer Fred Richens in 1938.

Refrigerators were required for storing fish and other perishables. Newer Frigidaire plant had been installed by the 1930s; previously each restaurant car carried considerable quantities of ice so as to keep food cool. Next to the kitchen the pantry contained a geyser to supply hot water for washing up, a coffee pot and, most importantly, a wine cellar. The wine list available to passengers compared 'favourably in class and variety with that of many hotels', the company reported. By the time the train left Brunel's great terminus at Paddington tables had been laid in the dining car ready for the first sitting; one difficulty was that staff did not know how many diners they might have to cater for, and while it was estimated that on a standard train as many as half the passengers using the dining car might be 'regulars', having lunch at the same day each week, it was left to the dining-car attendants and chef to manage the sittings to accommodate the other diners.

The work of the dining-car staff constituted something of a juggling act; without rushing diners, they had to ensure that the various courses were served in good time and that a sitting could be completed comfortably before the end of the journey, as travellers were 'inclined to be peevish if they have to desert an excellent meal because the train has arrived at their destination'. Regular travellers would often have a favourite seat and, in many cases, a favourite meal; this might be one not on the regular menu, but it was noted that 'any dish will be served at any time if

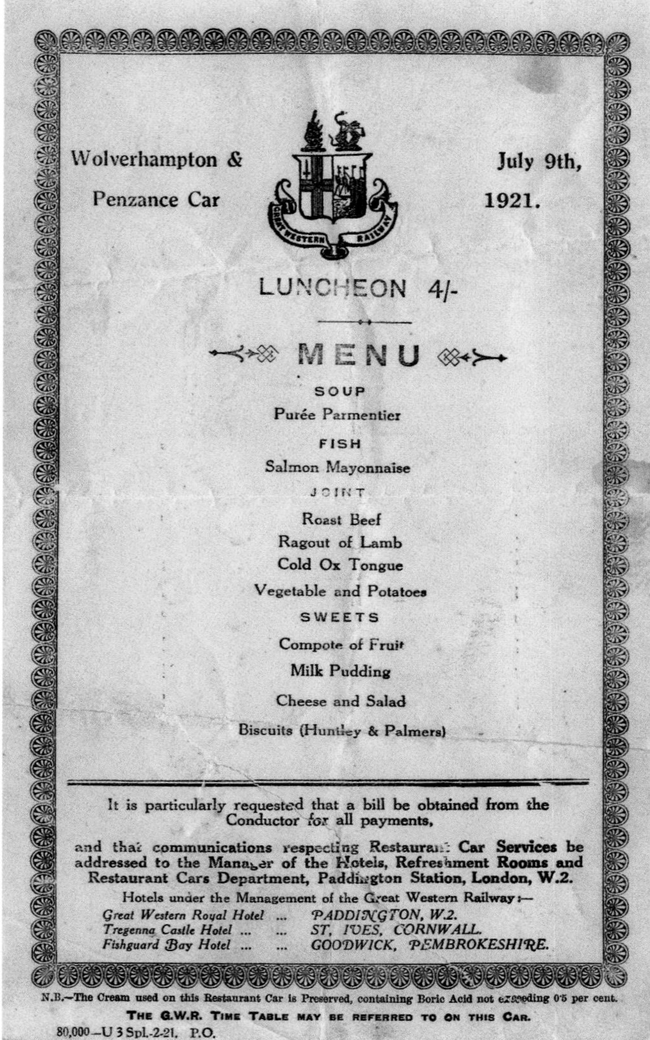

Wolverhampton & Penzance Car

July 9th, 1921.

LUNCHEON 4/-

MENU

SOUP
Purée Parmentier

FISH
Salmon Mayonnaise

JOINT
Roast Beef
Ragout of Lamb
Cold Ox Tongue
Vegetable and Potatoes

SWEETS
Compote of Fruit
Milk Pudding

Cheese and Salad

Biscuits (Huntley & Palmers)

It is particularly requested that a bill be obtained from the Conductor for all payments,

and that communications respecting Restaurant Car Services be addressed to the Manager of the Hotels, Refreshment Rooms and Restaurant Cars Department, Paddington Station, London, W.2.

Hotels under the Management of the Great Western Railway:—

Great Western Royal Hotel ... PADDINGTON, W.2.
Tregenna Castle Hotel ... ... ST. IVES, CORNWALL.
Fishguard Bay Hotel ... ... GOODWICK, PEMBROKESHIRE.

N.B.—The Cream used on this Restaurant Car is Preserved, containing Boric Acid not exceeding 0·5 per cent.

THE G.W.R. TIME TABLE MAY BE REFERRED TO ON THIS CAR.

80,000—U 3 Spl.-2-21. P.O.

ABOVE Two GWR chefs at work in the cramped confines of a busy restaurant car in the 1930s.

RIGHT GWR restaurant car menu.

notice is given' and the ingredients were on board. Care was also required on the part of the attendants in order to avoid accidents and spillages as, laden with plates, they made their way down the swaying dining car, serving dishes and condiments whilst avoiding passengers and other staff.

The company argued that dining-car menus had been designed to 'offer attractive meals yet preserve economy in management', and it retained specialist buyers at markets such as Covent Garden and Smithfield to ensure that only the best ingredients were used. An account of a journey in 1927 described a breakfast menu that included porridge, turbot, kippers and the traditional cooked breakfast of bacon and eggs; on the dinner menu were roast leg of mutton with a choice of vegetables, redcurrant jelly, cold ham and ox tongue, compôte of fruit, rice, custard, cheese and coffee. Just over a decade later the company was able to report that the 'increasing popularity' of ice cream meant that in the summer 'two-thirds of the passengers — including nearly all the ladies — regard it as the only fitting conclusion to a meal'.

The interwar development of new refreshment facilities at stations was mirrored by that of restaurant cars, the grander and more substantial dining cars, catering largely for First-class passengers, that had characterised the service in the early 1920s being gradually replaced by newer stock. In 1929 four new three-car dining sets were constructed for use on the 'Cornish Riviera Limited' and 'Torbay Limited'; each included a carriage that could seat 24 First- and 31 Third-class passengers, another housing the kitchens and pantry and a dining car catering for 64 Third-class passengers.

The changing tastes of travellers on the GWR were reflected in 1938 when the company heralded the introduction of five new 'buffet' cars, provided to 'meet the needs of passengers who require quick lunches, snacks or similar refreshments'. The modern, art-deco-style carriages were designed to have an 'inviting atmosphere' and a 'maximum of comfort', and as well as providing tables seating 20 diners they featured a long counter, behind which were a coffee machine and a bar. These vehicles followed the introduction of two 'Quick Lunch' carriages built at Swindon in 1934, the unique design of which featured a counter, running the whole length of the vehicle and with 12 stools, that could serve hot and cold snacks, sandwiches and fruit as well as 'tea and coffee, cocktails, ales, spirits and minerals and chocolate and minerals', according to the GWR's publicity. On-train meals, it was claimed, were 'the greatest of all assets to modern travelling' and resulted from 'much careful forethought and ingenuity' — something that could easily be said of the company's entire catering operation, which all year round supported the day-to-day success of the railway.

PART 4: AUTUMN

In a short article titled 'The Clocks Go Back' a correspondent in the *Great Western Railway Magazine* for October 1937 reflected on the end of summer, noting that railway staff who were at work at three o'clock in the morning of Sunday 3 October would 'call the bluff' of Summer Time and put the clocks 'back to normal'. Those on duty would, he mused, have the unusual experience of working an hour of their time all over again, while the rest of the population would sleep peacefully through it all. And while the beginning of autumn marked the end of the holiday rush, most notably the hustle-and-bustle of Saturday traffic, the new season did not mark a significant slackening of business for all departments, for a new set of challenges would concentrate the minds of management and staff in the months leading up to Christmas.

BELOW Winter travel on the Great Western. With carriage curtains drawn, neither of the models chosen by the GWR's publicity department for this 1930s photograph is displaying much enthusiasm for the rôle.

Autumn naturally saw the end of the summer timetables and the introduction of what the GWR called the 'winter train service'. Although trains that had been put on to meet the specific requirements of summer holiday traffic were withdrawn the company was usually in a position to announce some enhancements to its services over the autumn and winter period. An exception was 1926, when it found itself in a weakened financial position as a result of the General Strike, but a year later matters had improved, the 1927/8 winter timetable including the announcement that the 10.30am 'Cornish Riviera Limited' would be accelerated so as to reach Penzance at 4.55pm, five minutes earlier than hitherto. It also introduced a number of trains catering for the business community, among them a new 'Cheltenham Spa Express' scheduled to depart Paddington at 5pm and reach Cheltenham 2½ hours later, while similar trains 'that should prove of great value to businessmen' were timetabled to run between Paddington and both Reading and Birmingham.

The announcement of the 1932/3 winter service noted that 'with the cessation of summer tourist traffic the timetable will revert generally to that in operation during last winter, but will include some interesting improvements'. The new arrangements involved an acceleration of the 'Cheltenham Flyer', increasing its average speed to over 70mph, and the inclusion elsewhere on the network of a further 11 trains with a 'start-to-stop' average speed in excess of 60mph. West of England services, particularly those serving the Cornish resort of Newquay, were also enhanced, the 'Cornish Riviera Limited' making a new stop at Par, where coaches could be attached or detached, the journey time between London and Newquay being thus reduced by well over an hour. The 1932/3 winter timetable also saw the retention of Sunday services on the Birmingham–Stratford-upon-Avon line, 'affording facilities which have hitherto been available only during the summer period', according to the *Great Western Railway Magazine*.

Improvements notwithstanding, the printed timetables usually included a section giving details of lines, stations and halts that would be closed on Sundays over the winter. That applicable from 28 September 1936 to 4 July 1937 was no exception, listing more than

ABOVE **Passengers hurry past the carriage rank at Paddington on 5 September 1934. The lone hansom cab seems an anachronism in comparison with the group of motor taxis lined up ready for business.**

15 branch lines — many serving holiday resorts, such as Looe, Minehead, Par, Newquay and St Ives — and around 80 stations and halts all over the network, notably at Barry Island, Bridgnorth, Marazion and Porthcawl, none of which would be served on Sundays.

In 1935, its centenary year, the GWR announced that in the planning of its winter timetable attention 'had been given to increasing winter holiday traffic to the West of England'. Weekday and Sunday services were improved, and the new 'luxury' coaching stock introduced on the 'Cornish Riviera Limited' to coincide with the centenary was retained for use throughout the winter rather than being placed in store. The company produced a number of books promoting winter holidays, including *Winter in the West*, published in 1929, which asserted that 'the question is not so much shall we winter in the West as where shall we winter in the West?' It further argued that the Englishman had 'got into the groove of accepting August as his holiday month'. In *Winter Resorts*, produced five years later, in 1934, author Maxwell Fraser noted that while in many parts of England 'it was necessary to keep on the move in order to keep warm during the winter' there were 'favoured resorts' in the West Country where the whole atmosphere was 'strikingly different'. The secret was the Gulf Stream, which transformed the climate of the West Coast, Fraser argued, making it comparable with countries more than a thousand miles to the south. As well as a detailed descriptions of West Country resorts and their facilities the book contained 'Climatic and Medical Information' for many locations, to encourage travellers to visit. The entry for the Cornish resort of St Ives noted that its altitude was 300ft, its aspect 'North, South and East' and its climate 'mild but bracing', adding that this 'quaint and picturesque old-world spot makes an instantaneous appeal to those in search of peace and tranquillity' and that 'the climate is so equable that winter is practically unknown'.

The introduction of the winter timetables also required some work by station staff to ensure that the correct advertising

LEFT The front cover of a 1925 booklet issued by the GWR to promote its winter resorts and services.

material was on display. In a General Instruction notice issued by the Superintendent of the Line in September 1930 Mr R. H. Nicholls observed that 'at some stations pictorial posters are allowed to remain on the boards until they are very faded and not at all what they should be from an advertising point of view', adding that 'All concerned' should take the opportunity of the change from summer to winter services to take down poster boards and remove 'all cases of out-of-date, faded, dirty and torn bills' replacing them with current letterpress or pictorial posters. He then listed 10 posters that 'must be regarded as out-of-date', these including two advertising river trips on the Thames, one promoting Land Cruises and another featuring camping holidays on the railway.

Late summer and early autumn was also a period when the railway ran a great many special trains in connection with annual training exercises and camps run by the military. This traffic increased as international tension grew in the 1930s with the rise of Nazi Germany; the Bristol Diaries for 1937 note that over the year the company provided 80 special troop trains that between them carried more than 16,000 personnel, 414 horses and 738 guns and vehicles. Within this total the Great Western had run 14 special trains to support Territorial Army camps; many of these camps were in Berkshire and Wiltshire, and as a result, lines absorbed by the company in 1923, notably the Midland & South Western Junction Railway, saw increased levels of traffic. One such camp held at Ludgershall in 1930 saw the railway run 10 special trains in and nine out, conveying 116 officers, 2,200 men, 71 horses 41 vehicles and a staggering 89 tons of baggage. In that year well over 100 troop specials were run in the Bristol Division, 60 arriving at Lavington, where more than 10,000 officers and men and some 2,600 horses were dealt with, along with large quantities of luggage and stores. The Great Western also supported its own Territorial Army companies; in 1935 it was recorded that the 152nd (GW) Railway Construction Company, Royal Engineers, had a complement of 287 (a number that would increase in the years that followed), while the men attending the same year's annual camp at Longmoor reportedly spent a week on military training and a further fortnight practising bridge-building and track-laying.

The transportation of seasonal fruit and vegetables that had begun in spring continued throughout the summer and into the early autumn, when the traditional English fruit crops of apples and plums were harvested. A number of areas served by the GWR provided good business for the company in this regard, in particular the counties of Worcestershire, Herefordshire and Somerset. Recalling his time at Pershore in 1939, Harold Tupper described how the numbers of fruit wagons forwarded daily from the station grew from no more than a dozen in May to nearly 80 by late August. Pershore, in the Vale of Evesham, was famous for the 'Yellow Egg' plums that farmers had discovered growing wild in the early 19th century, as well as for the 'Pershore Purple', which appeared in the 1870s. Both varieties were popular with fruit farmers in the 1920s and 1930s, being suitable for cooking, canning and jam-making, while their firm skin allowed them to be transported over long distances without bruising.

The development of fruit-growing in the Vale of Evesham had been aided in no small part by good rail links with both Birmingham and London. The way in which plums were handled

BELOW A GWR covered fruit van, photographed on 14 October 1939. Labelled 'Empty to Evesham', it was used for plum traffic.

by the Great Western differed from the arrangements for strawberry traffic. Growers tended not to supply consumers or wholesalers direct, instead selling their produce to traders at the Co-operative and Central markets in Worcester. GWR staff from Pershore station were despatched to the markets each day to arrange the transportation of the fruit that had been purchased from farmers. GWR motor lorries from Worcester — and the Thornycroft delivery lorry from Pershore itself — were then pressed into service to carry fruit back to the station for despatch. Once unloaded in the goods yard the boxes of fruit were checked and consignment notes issued before the fruit was loaded into trains. Plums were also despatched from other local stations, including Evesham and Toddington, while from the 1890s sidings at Aldington, midway between Evesham and Littleton, provided extra capacity in order to relieve congestion at local stations in the plum season.

By the late 1920s fruit growers were beginning to feel the effects of increased competition from cheaper imported plums that arrived in the country by the middle of July; this naturally affected the GWR's revenue from handling such traffic, and the railway was faced with a further threat in the form of competition from road hauliers, who were able to transport fruit direct to large towns and cities without the need for additional loading and handling. In 1927, keen to support and promote local growers, the National Farmers' Union approached two GWR

ABOVE **'Bulldog' 4-4-0 No 3353 *Pershore Plum* — almost certainly the only GWR locomotive to be named after a fruit — at Shrewsbury in the 1930s.**

directors from the Worcester area — Stanley Baldwin and John W. Wilson — enquiring whether, as gesture of support to local farmers, the company would be willing to give one of its locomotives a name celebrating the centenary of the discovery of plums in the Vale of Evesham. Thus it was that 'Bulldog' 4-4-0 No 3353, built in 1900 and formerly named *Plymouth*, was renamed *Pershore Plum*. The locomotive was usually stabled at Worcester shed, being used on local trains in the Midlands, and was still at that depot when it was withdrawn in 1946.

Autumn also saw the harvest of another crop associated with Worcestershire and Herefordshire. Hops were 'the basis of our national beverage', noted the *Great Western Railway Magazine*, which reported that that of the 18,000 tons grown in Great Britain in 1935 more than 6,000 tons were produced in these two counties, Herefordshire ranking second only to Kent. The main areas for cultivation were those around Hereford itself, Ledbury, Withington, Ashperton and Stoke Edith. The picking season began at the end of August or the beginning of September, and in the space of one week the GWR was required to run a series of special trains to bring pickers into the area in readiness for the harvest. The pickers, more than three quarters of them women, numbered in excess of 20,000 and came from the mining areas of

South Wales, particularly around Aberdare, Merthyr Newport and the Rhondda, and from the West Midlands. The work was extremely hard, and pickers were paid according to the quantity of hops they could gather; once the harvest was complete the pickers returned home, the hops being dried in kilns before being despatched to market by train a few months later.

Many market towns served by the GWR held 'Mop' or hiring fairs on or around Michaelmas (29 September). Coinciding with the end of the harvest, such fairs dated back many centuries and presented an opportunity for farm workers and labourers to look for new employment as well as to celebrate and meet family and friends. By the 1930s the 'Mop' had become largely a social event and one that not only drew large numbers from the surrounding countryside but also attracted visitors from farther afield. The railway either ran special trains or offered cheap tickets for those attending fairs in market towns such as Banbury, Chipping Norton, Evesham, Marlborough, Stratford-upon-Avon, Tewkesbury and Warwick. In the case of the Gloucestershire town of Cirencester two handbills issued by the GWR in September 1934 reveal that cheap tickets 'at about the single fare for the double journey' were being offered from stations on both the Swindon–Gloucester line and the old Midland & South Western Junction route from Swindon to Cheltenham, trains terminating at the Town station of the Cirencester branch line or at Watermoor on the MSWJ route; late trains that departed after 10pm were provided on both routes to allow revellers to enjoy the stalls and fairground rides until late evening.

Cereal crops were also often harvested in late summer, and as a result the autumn was usually a busy time for one of the Great Western's less well-known facilities, the Provender Stores at Didcot. It was here that feed for the large numbers of horses used by the GWR was milled, mixed and prepared for distribution around the network. In the late 19th century this operation had been carried out at a converted goods depot at Handsworth in Birmingham, but this location was deemed to be too small to

BELOW Punnets of fruit being unloaded from rather grubby rolling stock at Paddington in the 1920s.

ABOVE **The exterior of the Provender Store at Didcot, photographed before the Great War. The reservoir seen in the foreground provided water for the store, the station and other GWR facilities nearby.**

cope with the growing number of horses then employed by the railway and was inconvenient and expensive to run. In 1882 the GWR board, after considering and rejecting the building of a second provender store at Paddington within the existing stable complex, agreed instead to build a brand-new facility close to the station at Didcot. The central location made ideal for the purpose, and, as the railway already owned the land, construction costs were kept to a minimum, although the imposing four-storey building, completed in 1884, nevertheless cost £160,000.

The main Provender Stores building was a steel-framed, brick-built structure located on land west of Didcot station and, being more than 200ft long and 72ft high, was an impressive facility. To produce the feed, hay and corn were lifted to the top floor by elevators for processing by chaff cutters. The floor below contained corn mills and chaff-sifters, while down another floor were the mixers, where feed was prepared to particular proportions specified by the company vet. Horses used by the GWR were fed with different mixtures of oats, beans, linseed, maize, hay and oat-straw depending upon the task they were required to perform; compared with those employed in towns and cities, those working at country stations were given a greater proportion of hay and fewer oats. The mix was also altered in the winter, the proportion of beans being increased in some cases, while special mixtures were prepared for nosebags and sick horses, according to a *Great Western Railway Magazine* article. Once mixed, the feed was delivered via a series of chutes to the ground floor, where it was bagged in readiness for despatch all over the system. It was estimated that a week's supply of feed for all the horses on the network amounted to more than 6,000 sacks, although well over double this number were in circulation in order to keep the whole operation moving.

The milling equipment and the heating system needed to dry the feed was originally powered by steam engines, but this antiquated system was replaced by electricity in 1901. Water for the mill was provided from steel tanks situated on two tall towers that dominated the local skyline, the water being drawn from a

reservoir at the west end of Didcot station; the same tanks supplied the station itself, as well as the goods yard and the locomotive depot. Not surprisingly, in view the raw materials involved, fire was a seen as a real threat to the safety of the building and its contents, and the water tanks also supplied a sprinkler system, which, the company argued, would 'make it practically impossible for a fire of any magnitude to occur'. The chimneys of steam locomotives shunting wagons into and out of the sidings serving the Provender Store were usually fitted with cowls to prevent any sparks from escaping; close to the building much of the shunting was carried out by horses, although in 1927 it was decided that these should be replaced by a petrol-engined Simplex locomotive, which was destined to remained in use until the mill closed in 1953.

The number of horses employed on the GWR, which in 1913 had exceeded 3,300, slowly declined in the years after the Great War as the company gradually introduced more motor vehicles. Even so, by 1930 there were still 2,499 horses in use, a figure that would be reduced to 1,687 seven years later. In the years before 1914 it was estimated that an area of over 9,000 acres was required to provide enough fodder for the railway's stock of horses; the directors were keen to 'purchase English instead of foreign oats', concluded the magazine article, and, as a result, supplies of corn, oats and maize were sought from farms all over

ABOVE Given the nature of the work carried out at the Provender Store and the fact that it was lit by large gas lamps like those shown here, it is little wonder that fire precautions were taken very seriously.

BELOW A GWR three-plank wagon full of hay bales for despatch to the Provender Store at Didcot. Local farms provided hay for the store for many years, although demand was such that the GWR had annually to look further afield for additional supplies.

ABOVE This view of the GWR goods warehouse at South Lambeth is of interest inasmuch as it features a number of railway horses, each with nosebag containing the mix of oats and other cereals prescribed by the company vet.

the GWR network and beyond. Consignments of feed were brought from sidings at the west end of Didcot station by the station pilot engine before being moved into the mill itself. Straw was also delivered in modified high-sided wagons and was required not only for mixing in feed but also in large quantities for bedding in stables located at GWR stations and depots. In 1937 a local newspaper reported that the Provender Stores at Didcot were producing 'everyday food' for 'hard-working horses' all over the GWR network and that it was, 'so to speak, generating many thousand horse power'. The article's apparent optimism turned out to be somewhat misplaced, however, the mill surviving for only eight years after the end of World War 2, although the building remained standing until 1967. (The site is now used as the main car park for Didcot station.)

Whilst the Provender Stores at Didcot provided feed for the horses in its ownership, used for humble tasks such as shunting and hauling delivery wagons, the Great Western also took care of rather more valuable thoroughbred racehorses — traffic that would disappear completely from the railway less than two decades after nationalisation. Horseboxes had been a feature of the raileway's passenger trains from its earliest days, when the transportation of horse-drawn carriages was commonplace. By the 1920s horsebox wagons were used for a variety of purposes, including the conveyance of working and farm horses, the movement of horses used by the military, and to transport racehorses to and from sales, studs and race meetings.

Until the advent of the railways horse racing had for the most part been a localised affair using unenclosed courses on common land. The railways transformed the 'sport of kings' into a national phenomenon, enabling horses, trainers, bookmakers and the general public to travel far greater distances to attend meetings. Racing became a spectator sport for the masses, and in the late-Victorian era larger and better-equipped enclosed courses, with grandstands and extensive catering facilities, sprang up all over the country. By the 1920s, when racing — like the railway — had recovered from the war, most horses and many punters still travelled to meetings by train. The GWR was ideally placed to benefit from interest in the sport, more than 20 of the country's largest and most important racecourses were being situated in its territory, among them Bath, Cheltenham, Chepstow, Newbury, Salisbury and Wincanton.

In addition to the courses there were a large number of training yards and studs based on the network. The Bristol Diaries record that in 1935 there were 66 'racehorse establishments' situated in the area covered by the Bristol Division and that 10,684 horses had been forwarded and received that year, generating an income in excess of £20,000. More than 40 stations in the division had handled racehorse traffic, although some had dealt with relatively modest numbers, such being the case at Frome, which handled a total of 41 horses; by contrast the two stations at Marlborough, at the heart of racing country on the Wiltshire Downs, had loaded and unloaded almost 1,300. The busiest stations for this traffic were all situated at the eastern extremity of the division, Challow, Shrivenham and Uffington between them handling more than 3,400 racehorses.

Less than 10 miles away, in the GWR's Reading Division, was the village of Lambourn, the history of which had been heavily influenced by the development of horse racing. Following the opening in 1898 of the Lambourn Valley Railway, an independent line built to link Lambourn with Newbury, horsebox traffic grew rapidly on the rather ramshackle branch, although the service was less than satisfactory until the operation was taken over by the GWR in 1905. Horsebox traffic reached its peak in the 1920s, when, on or before race days, large numbers of horses from the various training establishments around Lambourn would be loaded into horseboxes for their journey to racecourses all over the country. 'Race Special' trains, usually comprising a minimum of three or four horseboxes, were sometimes run on the branch, depending upon the volume of traffic; at Lambourn station staff could earn significant overtime if they were needed to load trains of this type on Sundays, when the branch was normally closed. If a special was not run, horseboxes were attached (usually at the rear) to scheduled passenger or parcels trains.

GWR instructions advised that, if possible, horseboxes should be arranged so that the horse would be travelling head-first, and,

BELOW Collett '2251' 0-6-0 No 2221 at Lambourn station on 2 September 1953. Four horseboxes are marshalled in the train, while another three can be seen in the siding. *T. C. Cole collection*

in view of the fact that racehorses tended to be extremely valuable and, in many cases, sensitive and highly strung, great care was taken in the loading process; the *General Appendix to the Rule Book* noted that 'if a horse is found to be restive from nervousness or any other cause, and there is a doubt of its travelling safely, the attention of the Station Master or other responsible person must be drawn to it'. In most cases someone from the stable would be on hand to assist and supervise GWR staff, and a stable lad or groom usually travelled in a compartment next to the horse for the duration of the journey. Guards were nevertheless instructed to check that horses were safely tethered at junction stations and at other locations *en route*. The horse was secured in the horsebox with two halter ropes, the *General Appendix* going so far as to stipulate the exact type of knot to be used by staff. Staff were also required to ensure that sufficient feed and water were available in the horsebox before departure, quantities varying according to the length of the journey. Besides assisting with the loading process station staff had to ensure that horseboxes were cleaned and disinfected before being used; it having been suggested that 'a prevalence of ringworm amongst racehorses might be due to inadequate cleansing of horseboxes', in 1937 the Superintendent of the Line was moved to write to stationmasters, requesting that mangers and horseboxes be 'properly cleansed'. Once they had been loaded the movement of horseboxes had to be handled with great care by train crews, both during shunting and on the journey itself; it was essential to avoid horses' being 'shaken or startled', stressed the GWR's instructions.

ABOVE The newly opened Newbury Racecourse station can be seen in this picture taken when the first meeting was held at the course, on 26/27 September 1905.

Although both flat and National Hunt racing remained popular in the 1930s the number of racehorses carried by the railway was beginning to decline. The first company to make road horseboxes available on a commercial basis was established in 1931, and trainers began to take advantage, initially for short journeys to local racecourses; over longer distances the railways still offered a quicker and safer service. In an attempt to regain the initiative the GWR introduced new horseboxes with improved springing and better ventilation. Accommodation for grooms and stable lads was also updated, with gas lighting and more comfortable seats, and a hatch was provided for checking on the condition of the horse during the journey. By 1938 the GWR was also offering very competitive rates for the transportation of horses taking part in races run under 'National Hunt, Jockey Club or Pony Turf Club rules', instructions issued in May of that year noting that, over distances of more than 150 miles, horses would be conveyed at just half the standard rate on the return leg of the journey.

A report on racehorse traffic in the Bristol Division in 1934 analysed the main reasons for a decrease in this business over the preceding decade; whilst snowy weather in 1927 and 1929 had been a serious factor in those years, from 1931 the decline was attributed to 'road competition'. In the 10 years from 1924 to 1934 the number of horses carried to race meetings had fallen from 10,384 to 4,600, the income generated decreasing by more than 50%. The statistics for the railway as a whole are striking but paint a similar picture. In 1923 the GWR carried 99,214 horses, a figure that increased to 108,542 two years later; by 1938 it had halved to 54,443. Trainers were increasingly attracted by the reductions in journey time offered by road operators; not only were there no delays at junction stations while horseboxes waited to be attached to connecting services, but the 'door to door' service provided by road competition also meant that stable lads no longer had to walk horses from racing establishments along country roads to stations and back again at the end of the return journey. In a further, belated effort to combat competition the Road Transport Department in 1936 began to offer a 'stable to station' service in and around Swindon and Marlborough, with a 'Road Motor Horse Box'. That year the lorry carried 111 horses, covering more than 700 miles while loaded but in excess of 1,400 empty, with the result that the income generated covered barely half the £80 operating costs.

Many of the horses carried on the Lambourn branch were transported a relatively short distance, to Newbury. The racecourse there held its first meeting on 26 September 1905, a station built to serve it opening the same day. By the 1930s the GWR was running excursions to Newbury from stations all over the network, including Paddington, Bristol, Newport and Cardiff. Two handbills issued by the company for a meeting on 26/27 October illustrate the different kinds of racegoer, the first promoting what the company termed a 'Restaurant Car Day Excursion', which drew passengers from South Wales and Bristol who were content to travel to the racecourse at a fairly leisurely pace, arriving just before 1pm (half an hour before the first race

BELOW Barely discernible at the extreme right, the date painted on the solebar reveals that this GWR horsebox had been outshopped by the Carriage & Wagon Works at Swindon in April 1937.

started), fares ranging from 18s First class to 10s Third; the second handbill, for a standard excursion from a similar catchment area, was aimed at a less-affluent clientèle, offering Third-class fares at 'a penny a mile'.

When, in 1906, the Great Western had built a new railway from Honeybourne to Cheltenham the route skirted the edge of the Cheltenham Racecourse at Prestbury. Unlike that at Newbury, which had been a new venture, the course at Cheltenham dated back to 1831, although steeplechasing had been introduced as recently as 1898, when the famous 'Gold Cup' was inaugurated. An agreement between railway and racecourse led to the establishment of a new station which opened in 1912, just in time for that year's Cheltenham Festival meeting. Set in a cutting, the facilities provided by the company were modest, comprising two platforms and a wooden ticket office; there being no sidings, racehorses were unloaded straight onto the platforms and walked up a ramp to the course. The station was open only on race days, but simple though the facilities were, it saved weary racegoers a long walk to or from either of the two main-line stations in Cheltenham. 'Travel Great Western Direct to the Racecourse Station', urged a GWR handbill promoting a race meeting in November 1934; 'the Great Western station is the ONLY station on the racecourse', it boasted, perhaps aiming a jibe at the LMS, which company's station at Lansdown, in the centre of Cheltenham, was some miles away.

ABOVE The interior of the groom's compartment of an ex-GWR horsebox, photographed at Didcot on 28 February 1955. Staff travelling with horses could look through the hatch on the right to check on the condition of their charges during the course of the journey.

Elsewhere the company provided excursion trains to race meetings all over the network; an account of a meeting at Bath in May 1925 recorded that around 1,100 reacegoers had been carried on special excursion trains from London and Cardiff, although heavy fog had delayed the beginning of proceedings, causing long delays to returning trains at the end of the day. Bad weather was unwelcome for GWR staff, as race excursions were often tightly timed; a handbill promoting an April 1923 excursion to Warwick from stations in the Swindon area (tickets costing 16s 6d for a First-class return and 9s 11d for a Third) advertised a 9am departure from Swindon and a noon arrival at Warwick, where the first race was timed to start at 2pm; the last race was due to start at 4.30pm, so punters would have had just half an hour to get back to the station before the return train left at 5.5pm. Special arrangements were made even at smaller race meetings; the Bristol Diaries for 1937 record that at that year's Easter Monday meeting at Wincanton just 200 passengers used the railway, arriving on scheduled services from Chippenham, Westbury and Weymouth. 'Road motor buses conveyed full loads from Bruton station to the racecourse and back, and buses left in good time for return trains,' reported the Divisional Superintendent.

Racing continued all year round, although steeplechasing began in late autumn, at around the same time as the fox-hunting season. Large numbers travelled to Badminton to see the Beaufort Hunt and via Faringdon to the Berkshire Hunt, and the GWR also transported hounds and horses where required. In 1922 the company was asked to make special arrangements for the Prince of Wales, who that year was to spend the hunting season at Easton Grey House, near Malmesbury. A hand-drawn map included within the Bristol Divisional Superintendent's annual report showed the distances to GWR stations from Easton Grey and revealed that although Tetbury station was only three miles away Badminton was a better choice because it was on the main line, allowing the Prince a speedier return to London when required. The Prince repeated the visit the following year and wrote to Viscount Churchill, the Company Chairman, expressing his 'sincere appreciation of all that has been done for me by the staff and employees of the Great Western Railway during my frequent journeys to and from the West Country' and stating that they had 'spared no effort to make such journeys comfortable in every way'.

Although horse racing had a sizeable following, sports such as rugby and football also drew large crowds on a weekly basis. In the 1920s and 1930s the football season did not normally begin

BELOW The Swindon Works J-Shop football team pictured in 1930.

ABOVE **The opening of the new GWR Staff Association building in Holbrook Street, Swindon, in 1932. The building included a 180-seat theatre, used by the Great Western Players for dramatic productions.**

until late August, by which time the cricket season was almost over; attendances at games were high, and thousands of supporters travelled to away games to watch their own teams. Few working-class people could yet afford to own a car, so rail travel was often the only way to get to matches. 'On Saturdays during the football season Cheap Day Return Tickets will be issued to Bristol by any ordinary train from stations within a rail distance of 60 miles,' noted a GWR timetable booklet for the 1934/5 season, the objective being to fill trains out of the holiday season. To drive the point home, when the company advertised cheap day returns to Bristol (and indeed other towns and cities on its network) sports fixtures always featured prominently; a 1934 handbill covering the period between October and the end of December advertised excursion tickets every Saturday from such stations as Shepton Mallet, Wells, Cheddar, Axbridge, Clevedon and Yatton to Bristol Temple Meads, listing the six fixtures being played by Bristol City at its Ashton Gate ground and a similar number for Bristol Rovers at the latter's Eastville stadium. Both teams were then in the Third Division (South) of the Football League but managed to attract respectable attendances; Third-class return fares were 2s 6d or less for the stations listed, return being permitted on any train later in the day.

Although keen to maintain business from football supporters on a week-by-week basis, when a team made good progress in a competition such as the FA Cup the railway usually gained increased revenue from important ties and particularly from finals. With a few exceptions most of the football teams based in towns and cities outside the capital were in the lower divisions, but on occasions they did well in knockout competitions. In January 1930 Swindon Town played Manchester City, company records noting that the railway carried 4,903 passengers to the game, including 230 away fans, and 270 from London. The game ended in a 1-1 draw, the GWR accordingly running a special to Manchester less than a week later for the replay at Maine Road. The 320 supporters who travelled north must surely have had a miserable return journey, having seen their team thrashed 10-1!

ABOVE **The Women's Section of the GWR Staff Association at Swindon, pictured in December 1939. Every possible activity thought likely to appeal to women is depicted, including flower-arranging, embroidery, sewing and basket-weaving. To complete the scene another member is bringing in a tray of tea!**

That football supporters were much less partisan in the 1930s becomes apparent from an account published in the company magazine for June 1938, describing special trains run for that year's FA Cup Final; more than 93,000 watched Preston North End beat Huddersfield Town 1-0 in extra time, and although neither team was located anywhere near the Great Western network the railway nevertheless ran 29 special trains carrying 12,150 fans to Paddington. It also catered for supporters of local clubs far removed from the higher echelons of the Football League, as evinced by a handbill issued in 1929 by the District Office at Oswestry. Three 'Half-day' excursions were run to Machynlleth, where the final tie of the Welsh Amateur Cup between Aberystwyth and Cardiff Corinthians was played on Saturday 20 April. The first train, carrying home supporters, ran direct from Aberystwyth, the second bringing passengers from inland stations such as Llanidloes, Newtown, Moat Lane and Caersws; the final train, originating from Portmadoc, called at Cambrian Coast stations, collecting supporters at such towns and villages as Harlech, Barmouth, Towyn and Aberdovey.

Rugby Union, arguably the national sport of Wales, provided a more partisan encounter which always generated plenty of business for the railway — the annual international game between England and Wales. This was held in alternative years at Twickenham and Cardiff and usually saw large numbers of supporters travelling by train. In January 1935 the match was played at Twickenham, and 22 specials were run by the GWR, among them seven 'well-loaded' trains from locations west of Cardiff and a further nine from the Welsh capital itself, an 'unprecedented number', it was reported. The 11,000 passengers transported by the company were part of a crowd that witnessed a 3-3 draw between the two old rivals, the scoreline ensuring that both sets of supporters returned home relatively happy.

For GWR employees who played competitive sport the end of summer and the start of autumn marked the beginning of the football and rugby season. The company encouraged and supported sporting, leisure and educational activities amongst its employees through the GWR Social & Educational Union, set up in 1923. This body had replaced the GWR Temperance Union, which had been wound up after 40 years, as, according to the *Great Western Railway Magazine*, 'intemperance had practically disappeared from the company's staff'. The Social & Educational Union sought to 'provide occasions and pursuits that would interest and educate its members'; it 'did not seek to spread its wings over any of the athletic, debating or musical bodies that were already in existence' but would help societies if they needed it. Its remit was very broad, and, along with its successor, the Great Western Staff Association, it supported many sports, including cricket, football, rugby, swimming, tennis, athletics, bowls and rifle shooting, in many cases at sports grounds and facilities provided by the railway itself. GWR staff teams participated in local leagues and also played 'All Line' matches between various divisions. In 1931 an 'international' football match played between English and Welsh GWR teams was held at Taunton, the away team winning 3-1. The company magazine reported that the Welsh team had 'deserved victory', owing to their superior ball control and passing. The 'All-Line' Rugby final played that year between Newport Docks and Carmarthen appeared to be a rather more competitive affair; resulting in a 19-18 win for Newport, the match was described as having been played in a 'keen but thoroughly sporting spirit'.

Throughout the season the company magazine provided accounts of all manner of sporting events; the annual GWR Swimming & Diving Gala held at Barry in September 1931 included a medley relay race for the Earl of Athlone Trophy, contested by 15 teams from all over the GWR network. The swimming final included two teams from Swindon Works, Plymouth, Neath and Newport Docks, the concluding event being an exhibition water-polo match between the local Barry amateur swimming club and a GWR Swindon team; the rather one-sided affair saw the railway team trounced 6-0. Other sporting events reported that year included an all-line Whist, Draughts & Skittles Championship held in Bristol in March, a skittles final fought out between Bridgwater Goods and Swindon Locomotive Factory and a low-scoring 'All-Line' cricket final between Cardiff and Taunton teams, played in September.

Railway staff participated in all manner of other leisure activities supported by the Social & Educational Union and, later, the Staff Association. The railway provided financial and practical support to both organisations over the years, enabling them to build and maintain institutes, meeting rooms and halls of all shapes and sizes for use by staff for educational and social activities. The work of the GWR Mechanics' Institute in Swindon is well known, but throughout the 1920s and 1930s many new facilities were opened elsewhere on the GWR network for the benefit of railway staff. A new institute opened in Swansea in November 1929 included a concert hall with large stage, under which was a large basement hall with kitchen and cloakroom which could be used for meetings. At the opening the directors of the company were thanked for 'the handsome way in which they had helped the branch to provide itself with a home'; the large premises would provide not only recreation for the 2,700 staff employed by the company in the town, it was noted, but also develop their talents in connection with education. Some years later a rather less grand facility, comprising a meeting room, cloakrooms and a skittle alley, was completed at Bridgwater; 'an atmosphere of irresistible happiness' was a feature of the opening ceremony, reported the *Great Western Railway Magazine*, and Assistant General Manager J. F. Lean took part in an inaugural skittle match with staff.

The social and educational events held in institutes and meeting rooms included drama, music, arts and crafts, 'fur and

BELOW The weekly programme for the Exeter branch of the Social & Educational Union, as reproduced in the *Great Western Railway Magazine* in 1928.

G.W.R. SOCIAL & EDUCATIONAL UNION

ASSEMBLY HALL

ST. THOMAS, EXETER

Programme for Week commencing January 12th

Day	Event	Commencing hour	Price of Admission
Monday January 12th	Dance – Triopheans Band. Prizes for Spot Dances - Novelties	8 to 11 pm.	9d
Tuesday 13th	Monster Whist Drive. Top prize – £5.	8 pm	1/-
Wednes. 14th	Variety & Entertainment. Proceeds - Helping Hand Funds.	7-30 pm.	1/- 6d & 3d.
Thurs. 15th	Popular Concert - Orchestra - Vocal & Instrumental Solos -	8 pm	6d & 3d.
Friday 16th	Grand Social – Games-Music-Dancing Competitions - Refreshments	7.45 pm.	1/- Inclus:
Saturday 17th	Monster Whist Drive. Top prize – £5	8 pm	1/-

ALL ARE WELCOME

A. W. TOWELL, Entertainment Hon. Sec.
T. D. WILLIS, Branch Hon. Sec.

feather' and horticultural and floral exhibitions, as well as social gatherings. The *Great Western Railway Magazine* reported widely on these activities every month; the December 1938 edition carried a full account of the 12th annual GWR Arts & Crafts Exhibition, held at Paddington station. For variety and excellence of work and originality of design the exhibition was 'definitely the finest of the series', it was noted. There were more than 200 entries in the Painting & Sketches category; it was reported that Swindon artist Hubert Cook 'dominated the portrait class' with his group of 'well-constructed' studies. Cook worked as a machinist in Swindon Works until 1944 and went on to become an accomplished professional artist. The show also included a photographic section, 'the largest ever staged in the exhibition, but undoubtedly the best', the article concluded. Entries in the needlework and embroidery section 'paid testimony to the very high level of ability of women exhibitors' and included all manner of needlework as well as items of 'everyday utility'. There were also 'well-filled classes' for knitted articles such as jumpers, cardigans and pullovers 'of plain and fancy design'; in addition examples of leatherwork, gloves, wicker, cane and rugs and mats were shown. Many railwaymen, especially those employed in the Locomotive, Carriage & Wagon Department, excelled at the more practical hobbies such as woodwork, metalwork and model-making, and medals were awarded for the best work.

Music was another an important part of the leisure activities of GWR staff, many of whom participating in concerts and performances, as individuals and in groups; there were numerous choirs and music groups of all types who played at both local events and special occasions, such as summer and Christmas concerts. The highlight of the year was the GWR Annual Musical Festival, which by the 1930s ran over three days of competition and included well over 1,000 entrants entered in more than 40 different classes. These included male-voice and mixed choirs, vocal solo performances, orchestra, string and woodwind instruments and piano, but prizes were also given for non-musical activities, such as elocution, public speaking, debating, poetry and essay-writing. Drama was similarly popular with staff, and many enthusiastic amateur groups performed at GWR events, competition and festivals. The second annual performance by the GWR Social & Educational Union Shakespearean Society at St Paul's Hall, Paddington, in 1930 elicited a rather mixed review in the company magazine; 'Much Ado About Nothing' reportedly 'maintained the interest of the audience', the comedy being 'generally good' and the drama 'fair', but the piece concluded with the observation that 'the players would be well advised to remember not to commit the unpardonable error of making emphasis in the wrong places'.

Another regular event in the calendar in relation to staff leisure activities were the 'Fur & Feather' shows organised locally and across the GWR network. These competitions usually included classes covering a wide range of domesticated animals and birds, as well as produce; a show held in September 1931 by the railway's Exeter Division included 62 entries covering poultry, bantams, pigeons, rabbits, cage birds and fruit and vegetables, prizes being distributed by one of the company's directors. The 'All-Line' Fur & Feather Show held in Bristol a month later attracted 'fanciers from a large number of stations' and more than 500 entries. On this occasion prizes were presented by the Assistant Goods Manager of the GWR, who remarked that the exhibits 'were a revelation' and that interest in the show was 'indicative of the cooperative spirit in off-duty conditions' and he felt that 'the same spirit ran through the actions of staff whether at work or play'. The prize for the best cage bird was awarded to an employee at Swindon Works, while Mr Griffiths of Oswestry won a trophy for his Rhode Island Red hen.

Underlying many of the activities carried out under the auspices of the Social & Educational Union and the Staff Association was a determination to raise money for the 'Helping Hand Fund'. Set up in 1924, the fund provided assistance for GWR staff and their families who found themselves in difficulties. Staff could opt to have a sum taken from their weekly pay, but there were also collecting boxes provided at many locations, and an article in the *Great Western Railway Magazine* for November 1931 noted that donations had been received from boxes at locations as diverse as Helston and Shrewsbury. Other funds came from a variety of other sources. Each month the company magazine published a list of contributions from members of the Social & Educational Union and other GWR staff; the February 1929 issue included a list of more than 120 separate donations that included a gift of £13, the proceeds of a dance held by the Newbury branch, £29 collected from the railway works and offices at Swindon and 10s collected at a Christmas rally at Southall locomotive shed. The list of contributions was usually accompanied by details of how the money had been used; on this occasion the magazine reported that 48 'cases of distress' had been brought to the notice of the fund, and assistance given amounting to more than £160.

'With the advent of winter evenings, large numbers of Great Western employees will this month devote themselves to courses of studies calculated to increase their efficiency in their work and their usefulness to the community,' wrote a correspondent in the *Great Western Railway Magazine* in 1929. The company actively supported vocational training, and in November that year it was noted at a board meeting that it had arranged various lectures and correspondence courses in subjects such as law, signalling, station accountancy and arithmetic. It also had arrangements with local councils to provide other training, in subjects such as book-keeping and shorthand. Railway management also supported the work of Lecture & Debating societies in Bristol, Swindon and London, which held regular meetings to consider transport-related topics.

Between the two world wars the commemoration of the signing of the armistice ending the Great War continued to be an

ABOVE **Mrs W. Parr of Paddington is awarded a cup for knitting at the Swindon Arts & Crafts Exhibition in 1952. Behind the judging panel can be seen all manner of artwork and models.**

important part of the railway calendar. The first formal ceremony was held at Paddington in November 1919, as it was at many other locations. That year the stationmaster and around 200 staff took part, the *Great Western Railway Magazine* reporting that 'bareheaded, the men stood before the memorial while the impressive silence ruled over the great terminus'. The ceremony grew larger each year, and in 1922 a new, larger war memorial was unveiled. A vicar from the local parish church of St James in Paddington normally officiated, members of the GWR Choral Society providing a musical accompaniment. This arrangement was less helpful when 11 November fell on a Sunday, as it did in 1928, the curate standing in for the vicar and the choral society not present in large numbers, as its many of members had duties in local choirs. Surviving GWR correspondence notes that a harmonium had to be borrowed from St James for the ceremony but that this was 'not as convenient'.

The 'General Instructions' issued weekly by the GWR usually gave details of ticketing arrangements for the Armistice Day events held on 11 November each year; the 1938 circular noted that reduced-fare tickets were to be issued to members of the British Legion and their families travelling to London for the annual parade and ceremony at the Cenotaph and the Festival of Remembrance held at the Albert Hall that evening. As now, poppies were sold to mark Armistice Day, although collections were made on a rather more limited basis than today; a GWR circular issued in 1930 stated that, in connection with the annual collection on behalf of the Earl Haig Fund, stationmasters 'may give permission for collections to be made on the Company's premises, on condition that Waiting Rooms and trains standing at platforms are not entered'.

The first signs of Christmas on the GWR were apparent not in its stations but at the docks it operated, particularly those in South Wales. Around three weeks before the festivities goods from 'Empire and Overseas markets' were unloaded and despatched to London and other provincial centres where they would be distributed from warehouses. In October, November and early December freight-train mileage was generally high. The writer of an article in the *Great Western Railway Magazine* for December 1937 described the 'seasonal cargoes' being carried on the railway, these including 'oranges, apples, lemons, grapes, bananas, dried fruits, nuts, mistletoe, holly, meat, poultry, livestock, wines, toys of all descriptions, crackers and a host of miscellaneous articles'. The traditional British Christmas lunch necessitated the running of special trains transporting refrigerated meats, notably beef, chicken and turkey, between the countryside, GWR ports and cold storage facilities. A large proportion of the meat and poultry consumed at Christmas between the two world wars was imported from Ireland, and in addition to the company's own cross-channel services between Rosslare and Fishguard others were operated between Cork and Fishguard to cope with the demand. Once unloaded at the West Wales port, meat and poultry was transported direct to London in special 'perishable' trains, to ensure prompt delivery.

The Christmas period has always traditionally been the busiest time of year for the Post Office, its staff handling millions of parcels, letters and greetings cards, and in the 1920s and 1930s the demands placed on the GWR to convey much of this postal and parcels traffic were intense. Matters came to a head in the week preceding the holiday, and an article in the December 1937 *Great Western Railway Magazine* reported that 'for many weeks past there has been the closest collaboration between the Company and the Post Office'. Detailed planning ensured not only that special trains were provided to cope with the extra business but also that existing services were strengthened with additional coaches during the peak period before Christmas. In 1938 it was noted by the company that 'the very heavy parcels traffic' necessitated the running of 90 special trains during the Christmas period.

To relieve the pressure on the already busy parcels office at Paddington the nearby Alfred Road depot was 'specially used'

BELOW **Unloading the Christmas mail at Paddington in 1926.**

for dealing with the estimated 65,000 bags of parcels and mail despatched from the London area via the GWR. As well as dealing with domestic mail and parcels the Great Western handled large quantities of overseas mail that arrived at Plymouth before the festive season. In 1937 five liners called at the port, three, including the *Queen Mary*, bringing mail from the United States, and two others parcels and post from China, Japan and India. The same year it was reported that at Bristol Temple Meads 30 'supernumeraries' were being employed to cope with the 'Christmas parcel rush'. In order to deal with parcels and luggage in the weeks leading up to Christmas additional platform trolleys were often required, and these could be borrowed from the General Stores at Swindon Works. Inevitably the return of the trolleys was not quick enough for the authorities at Swindon, and the General Instructions issued by the company to staff each January in the 1920s and 1930s include much the same note, urging staff to return trolleys and trucks 'forthwith', stationmasters being requested to give the matter their 'personal attention'.

ABOVE Christmas decorations at Paddington in December 1935, including a giant Christmas cracker reminding travellers that the GWR was celebrating its centenary. In the distance can be seen the entrance to the Great Western Royal Hotel, which allowed travellers direct access from the 'Lawn'.

Some of the parcels handled by the GWR each Christmas may well have contained gifts of some of the publicity material and books it produced. Every year in the weeks before Christmas the 'General Instructions' circular sent to staff included a list of the company publications then in print, along with a request to 'do what is possible to foster sales'. As an incentive employees were offered a commission of a half-penny on 6d sales, 2d on 1s sales and 10% commission on sales above 1s, being urged to 'order early for Christmas'. Also listed were jigsaw puzzles, aimed at 'boys and girls of all ages', which had been marketed and sold by the GWR since 1924; by the late 1930s more than 750,000 had been sold, and an article in the company magazine boasted that the puzzles were 'the most popular' then on the market and still represented great value at the 'ridiculously low' price of half a crown. Forty different designs had been produced, although by the late 1930s only around half this total were still available. The editor noted that 'Christmas is almost upon us', adding that 'your children, your nephews, nieces and friends must have presents' but concluding: 'Perhaps you haven't given yourself a present for a very long time. Here is the very thing.'

Whether GWR jigsaw puzzles were on sale at two Christmas displays organised by department stores in Bristol and London and supported by the Great Western's own publicity department is unconfirmed, although it seems highly likely that they would have been. In November 1938 the Christmas Bazaar at Maggs' in Bristol featured a reproduction of a GWR locomotive cab, complete with sound effects, manned by female shop staff dressed in overalls and caps loaned by the company. The *Great Western Railway Magazine* reported that 'posters and other publicity material also helped create a railway atmosphere' and that the attraction was 'symbolic of the modern Father Christmas's reindeer and sleigh'. At the other end of the GWR main line a 'North Pole Express' display at Morley's in London featured a real GWR carriage that had been converted into a cinema showing alternate journeys on film, one to the North Pole and the other to the Cornish Riviera, children being subjected to the company's film 'Cornwall — the Western Land'. Quite what unsuspecting children expecting to see Santa made of it all is not recorded.

Christmas decorations had been erected on the 'Lawn' at Paddington for the first time in 1934 and proved popular enough to become an annual feature. In 1937 the company magazine reported that roof pillars were to be turned into large candles which would be lit in various colours; above them the roof was to resemble a 'star-spangled sky', a large illuminated lantern being hung in the centre of the space and a Father Christmas figure 'ensconced' on the roof of the sales kiosk; all these decorations would appeal to the thousands of pupils who passed through the station on their way home from the various public schools that were located around the GWR system. That year the bulk of the students returning to the capital arrived at Paddington on 21 December, special trains being run from Dartmouth, Marlborough, Malvern and the Bristol area, students from Taunton having arrived a few days earlier. A few years earlier, in 1931, this annual traffic warranted a mention in the annual report submitted by the Divisional Superintendent at Bristol, who recorded that in connection with the Marlborough College Christmas vacation special trains were run from Marlborough (Low Level) station to Paddington via Swindon on 17 December, no fewer than six breakfast cars providing sustenance for the scholars on their way home. Two days later further specials were run for students from Clifton and Bath, restaurant-car facilities being provided on the trip to Paddington. The railway also offered cheap tickets for older students sitting entrance examinations at Oxford and Cambridge, which in the 1930s took place immediately after the Christmas vacation, in the first week of January; a company circular issued in December 1932 noted that tickets could be issued in advance of the holiday period for students sitting examinations at Brasenose, Christchurch, Jesus, Lincoln, Merton and Oriel colleges on 3 January.

For the bulk of the population train travel at Christmas served a number of other purposes. In the weeks before the festivities people were keen to use trains to travel to towns and cities to shop and go to the cinema, theatre and music-hall shows and other Christmas events. A programme advertising 'cheap day ticket arrangements from Bristol and Suburban Districts' issued by the GWR in the autumn of 1934 listed such attractions as classical concerts at the Colston Hall, revues at the Little Theatre and Central Hall, 'Talkie Theatres' and pantomimes at the Prince's Theatre and Theatre Royal. Excursion booklets and handbills issued by the GWR at this time of year not only highlighted the various attractions on offer for travellers but also offered cheap tickets as an incentive. In addition to normal cheap day excursion tickets, in the 1930s the company heavily promoted 'Penny-a-mile' summer tickets, which could be used before, during and after the Christmas holidays for travel between all stations by any advertised train, return being permissable at any time up to a month later.

The GWR's ever-resourceful publicity department provided a Christmas-gift idea for travellers that could also be an incentive to use the railway; in 1936 it introduced 'Christmas and New Year Gift Tickets', a facility allowing people to send greetings cards containing railway tickets to relatives and friends, inviting them to visit in the holiday period. Instructions issued to staff the following year noted that bookings could be made during the period 11 December 1937 to 8 January 1938 for travel between any two points served by one of the 'Big Four' railway companies (including joint lines). The idea was imaginative, but the application process was rather tortuous; once a request for tickets had been made at a GWR station or booking agency a letter was sent to Paddington with all the relevant details, and only when the application had been processed were the greetings card and tickets sent then back to the station, where they could be paid for and collected by the customer.

In an era before mass car ownership railway travel at Christmas time was primarily to return home for the holiday or to visit friends or family. Not surprisingly, the busiest period for the GWR was normally Christmas Eve, when thousands of people were travelling home. 'Christmas is no holiday for the railwayman', noted a headline in the *Bristol Evening World* in December 1937, the accompanying article reporting that passenger traffic in the West that year was expected 'to reach even greater proportions than it did last Christmas'. Some of the most important express services, such as the 'Cornish Riviera Limited', were run in several portions to cope with high passenger numbers, much as they were on busy summer Saturdays, the Bristol newspaper article

reporting that 'many of the ordinary trains will be run in duplicate or triplicate and even, in some cases, in four parts'. Traffic to South Wales from both London and Bristol was also heavy, particularly in the 1930s — a reflection of the hard times experienced by the region during the Depression, which had prompted so many people from that area to move to London in search of work. Trains and stations were crowded, but thanks to the provision of additional trains and the hard work of GWR staff most passengers were able to complete their journey in time for Christmas. 'One cannot but be impressed by the jollity and good humour of the passengers,' noted a correspondent in the December 1937 *Great Western Railway Magazine*, who added that 'for the most part they are extremely tolerant' and that 'Mr Scrooge would find it difficult indeed to find many kindred spirits among the happy and excited thousands who invade Paddington on Christmas Eve'.

Although some trains ran on Christmas Day, traffic was usually very light; GWR locomotive driver Gordon Shurmer recalled a trip on Christmas Day 1945 down the old Midland & South Western

ABOVE **Paddington station at 11am on 11 November. As the Act of Remembrance takes place further down Platform 1 male passengers stand bare-headed, observing the two-minute silence.**

Junction route from Swindon to Andover via Marlborough during which no passengers got on or off at any of the stations throughout the entire journey. As Gordon remarked, 'Who would want to spend their precious holiday on a draughty Wiltshire platform, waiting for a stopping train to Andover?' Traffic was, however, traditionally much heavier on Boxing Day. Special late trains were provided, as 26 December was traditionally a day when, as well as visiting relatives, many people attended football and rugby matches in great numbers, and late return trains enabled revellers and supporters to make the most of their day. A GWR handbill advertising such trains from Bristol on Boxing Day in 1934 recorded that the last return service to stations on the North Somerset line to Radstock, Midsomer Norton and Frome left Bristol Temple Meads as late as 11.20pm, giving passengers ample chance to see relations or enjoy Bristol's night life. Another typewritten circular, giving details of special trains between Yeovil and Taunton in the same period, noted that late services would also run to serve both locations as well as smaller stations in between, such as Durston, Athelney and Montacute. The normal timetable was subject to considerable change on Boxing Day, and the printed winter timetables issued by the company each year usually included a list of trains that would be subject to alteration or suspension; the 1936 timetable included two pages of changes to affecting more than 100 main-line and cross-country trains, many early-morning departures being cancelled, for obvious reasons. There were also alterations to the steamship services operated by the company; on 26 Decemnber 1938 there was no night-time sailing from Fishguard to Rosslare or from Fishguard to Waterford, although sailings to the Channel Islands were maintained as normal.

Business usually remained brisk after the holiday; in the 1920s and 1930s the more affluent increasingly chose to stay 'in any number of beautiful resorts in the West of England where Winter may be enjoyed instead of suffered' over the Christmas period, and, as the GWR's publicity noted, an improved winter timetable and the provision of seasonal entertainment at holiday destinations ensured 'a jolly time in ideal surroundings'. Rather less jolly were the large numbers of conferences and residential meetings organised between Christmas and the New Year. Each year circulars issued by the Superintendent of the Line noted the courses and conferences for which reduced fares had been arranged. This being the school holiday period, a goodly number of educational and teaching-union conferences were held at this time of year; in 1929 conferences for the National Union of Teachers and the National Union of Women Teachers and a meeting of the Science Masters' Association were just three of the events for which cheap tickets were offered.

As the post-Christmas period was also the traditional pantomime season the Great Western worked closely with theatre managers and promoted excursion tickets that combined both a rail and theatre ticket. In 1937 special arrangements were made with two theatres in Birmingham to enable families travelling from stations in the West Midlands to see either 'Mother Goose' or 'Goody Two Shoes'; a similar excursion was offered in connection with performances of 'Dick Whittington' at the New Theatre in Oxford.

For many children no pantomime trip was complete without an ice cream, and instructions issued to GWR staff in 1938 reminded them that 'Messrs J. Lyons & Co anticipate despatching quantities of Ice Cream traffic ... to cinemas, theatres, cafes etc in the provinces during the Christmas period,' adding that the 'best arrangements' should be made to ensure 'expeditious transits and deliveries'. If ice cream arrived by train after the station delivery van had departed on its round a special delivery was to be arranged if possible; there being no refrigerated storage facilities at stations, melting ice cream was a very real prospect and one that could lead to claims from suppliers.

By contrast station staff were asked not to deliver any goods to the stores of F. W. Woolworth & Co in the period between Christmas Day and New Year's Day, during which time they would be completing their annual stock-take. The only exceptions to this instruction were, noted a GWR circular, foodstuffs and perishables supplied daily to stores and cafés, and New Year greetings cards, which were to have consignment notes marked 'Deliver Immediately'. Other goods destined for Woolworth stores was to be held in depots and sheds during the holiday period. 'As much traffic as possible' was to be delivered on 2 January, and store managers were to be consulted if this proved impracticable.

The return of pupils at the start of the new school term in January marked the end of the Christmas rush on the Great Western; for staff there would have been little opportunity for a break at Christmas, most being hard at work over the holiday period. They could, however (as the company noted in 1937), be 'relied on to give of their best to the thousands of people who, directly and indirectly, look to them to provide one of the essential services' in the festive season. Christmas and New Year over, they could look forward once more to the promise of spring and another busy summer.

RIGHT A Christmas grotto at the front of the 'Lawn' at Paddington in December 1956. The displays were in support of a collection for the Greater London Fund for the Blind.

SCOT
GAS WATER HEATERS
MMEDIATE & ONSTANT
HOT WAT
SEE THEM AT YOUR
GAS SHOWROOMS
ASCOT
ARRIVAL INDICATOR
NOW IS THE TIME
INVEST IN
WESTBOURNE PARK
BUILDING SOCIETY
YMANS
STOP!
LOOK!
GIVE!
IT'S
HELP
THE
BLIND
vening" Paper

ACKNOWLEDGEMENTS

As always, I am grateful to the staff at a number of libraries and archives for their assistance during the research for this book, in particular the National Archive at Kew, Bristol Central Library and Swindon Central Library. Special thanks are due to Elaine Arthurs, Collections Officer at the STEAM Museum in Swindon, for making available archive material from the library there and also for her hard work in sourcing images for inclusion the book. I should also like to acknowledge the ongoing assistance of the volunteers past and present at the STEAM Museum library, David Hyde, Peter Rance of the Great Western Trust, Phil Kelley, Richard Abbey, Alan Wakefield and Rosa Matheson. Colleagues at the British Motor Industry Heritage Trust also provided valuable support, and I should particularly like to thank Lisa Stevens and Gillian Bardsley for their assistance. Thanks are due also to Nick Grant and Kevin Robertson at Ian Allan Publishing for their patience and support during the somewhat prolonged completion of the book. It could not, however, have been completed without the support of my family, and I want to thank Clare, Liz, Jack and Katie for their encouragement, as always. Finally, I must acknowledge the assistance of my wife, Ann, who as usual read and edited the text and provided the love and support I needed to finish the book.

BIBLIOGRAPHY

Much of the primary material used in this book was drawn from Great Western Railway 'RAIL' files held in the National Archives at Kew. Other information was sourced from the library at the STEAM Museum in Swindon, the Great Western Society at Didcot and the local collection of Swindon Central Library. Space does not permit the listing of individual circulars, handbills and instructions issued by the company and mentioned in the book, but much information was drawn from the following:

GWR Board minutes
GWR Traffic Committee minutes
GWR Chief Officers Conference minutes
GWR Hotels & Refreshment Committee minutes
GWR Circulars & General Instructions 1930-1939 (RAIL 253/513)
GWR Excursion handbills 1929 (RAIL 253/469)
GWR Miscellaneous excursion handbills 1937 (RAIL 253/472)
GWR Special matters dealt with; Traffic Notices, Receipts and other matters, Bristol Division (The Bristol Diaries) 1913-1939 (various RAIL 253 file numbers)

GWR official publications

Conveyance of Agricultural, Farm & Dairy Produce, April 1925
Commerce and the Great Western Railway, April 1924
General Appendix to the Rule Book, August 1936
General Statistics, 1938
Great Western Ports, 1929
The GWR Guide to Economical Transport, 1936
GWR Hotels & Catering — Tariffs and General Arrangements for Travellers, 1929
Holiday Haunts (various editions)
Instructions for Signalling Trains during fogs and falling snow and in frosty weather, October 1923
Look Out! Some Hints for Permanent-Way Men, 1936
The 10.30 Limited, 1923
Track Topics —A GWR Book of Engineering, 1935
Winter Resorts on the GWR, 1934

Published works

Allen, J.: *The Berks & Hants Line: Theale to Bedwyn* (D. & M. Canning, 2001)
Bennett, A.: *The Great Western Railway in West Cornwall* (Kingfisher Publications, 1988)
Bennett, A.: *Great Western Lines & Landscapes* (Runpast Publications, 2002)
Bryan, T.: *The Inheritance — The Great Western Railway between the Wars* (Ian Allan Publishing, 2013)
Fenton, M.: *The Malmesbury Branch* (Wild Swan Publications, 1999)
Gardner, J.: *Brunel's Didcot* (Runpast Publications, 1996)
Jordan, A. & E.: *Away for the Day — The Railway Excursion in Britain* (Silver Link Publishing, 1991)
Karau, P.: *GWR Branch Line Termini* (Oxford Publishing Co, 1974)
Kelley, P.: *Great Western Road Vehicles* (Oxford Publishing Co, 2002)
Maggs, C.: *Bristol Railway Panorama* (Millstream Books, 1990)
Matheson, R.: *The Swindon 'Trip' — The Annual Holiday for Swindon Works* (History Press, 2006)
Pixton, R.: *Oxford, Worcester & Wolverhampton — Portrait of a Famous Route* (Runpast Publications, 2003)
Pole, F. J. C.: *His Book* (Town & Country Press, 1968)
Price, M. R. C.: *The Lambourn Valley Railway* (Oakwood Press, 1964)
Russell, J.: *Great Western Company Servants* (Wild Swan Publications, 1983)
Russell, J.: *Great Western Horse Power* (Oxford Publishing Co, 2010)
Russell, J.: *Great Western Carriages* Volumes 1 and 2 (Oxford Publishing Co, 1972 and 1973)
Russell, J. H.: *A Pictorial Record of Great Western Wagons* (Oxford Publishing Co, 1971)
Russell, J. H.: *Freight Wagons and Loads in service on the GWR and British Rail Western Region* (Oxford Publishing Co, 1989)
Timms, P.: *Working at Swindon Works 1930-1960* (Amberley Press, 2014)
Vaughan, A.: *The Great Western at Work 1921-1939* (PSL Books, 1993)
Vaughan, A.: *The Great Western's Last Year* (History Press, 2013)
Semmens, P. W. B.: *The Heyday of GWR Train Services* (David & Charles, 1990)
Wragg, D.: *GWR Handbook* (Haynes Publishing, 2010)

Journal and magazine articles

Many of the activities noted within this book were reported in the *Great Western Railway Magazine* during the period 1918-39. Other sources consulted were as follows:

Bennett, A.: 'Fish Traffic from Cornwall' (*Railway World*, October 1983)

Clark, B.: 'Railway Gardens' (*Backtrack*, May/June 1991)

Copsey, J.: 'Horse Box Traffic on Passenger Trains' (*Great Western Journal* No 5, Winter 1993)

Copsey, J.: 'Whitland Milk Train in Postwar Years' (*Great Western Journal* No 35, Summer 2000)

Esbester, M.: 'The Safety Movement' (*Great Western Echo*, Autumn 2008)

Fenton, M.: 'Christmas Day on the MSWJR' (*Great Western Journal* No 41, Winter 2002)

Jenkins, S.: 'The St Ives Branch' (*Great Western Journal* Special Cornish Issue, 1992)

Lewis, J.: 'GWR Horse Traffic and Horseboxes Part 2' (*Great Western Journal* No 78, Spring 2011)

Pugh, B. E.: 'Fog Working' (*Great Western Journal* No 32, Autumn 1999)

Riley, R. C.: 'Steam on the "Broccolo"' (*Trains Annual* 1966)

Tupper, H.: 'Pershore Fruit & Vegetable Traffic' (*Great Western Journal* No 26, Spring 1998)

Williams, T.: 'An Introduction to the GWR Permanent Way Department' (*Great Western Journal* No 45, Winter 2003)

INDEX

ABOVE A 'Star' 4-6-0 awaits departure from Paddington on the evening of 19 April 1938.